# CHESAPEAKE
# OYSTERS

*To Benjamin Ford and Meghan Livie: every word of this book was possible
because of your love, support, patience and inspiration.
I can never thank you enough, for everything.*

*And to the memory of Scott Livie, who gave me my first oyster,
and shared his love of the Chesapeake Bay with me.
I love you, Dad. You were with me all along the way.*

*The largest genuine Maryland oyster—the veritable bivalve of the Chesapeake...is as large as your open hand. A magnificent, matchless reptile! Hard to swallow? Dangerous? Perhaps to the novice, the dastard. But to the veteran of the raw bar, the man of trained and lusty esophagus, a thing of prolonged and kaleidoscopic flavors, a slow sipping saturnalia, a delirium of joy!*

—H.L. Mencken, 1913

# CONTENTS

# INTRODUCTION

He was a bold man," asserted Jonathan Swift, "who first ate an oyster." Swift was right—oysters are unlikely additions to our culinary customs. Fortressed in their thick shells, more closely resembling rubble than food, it's a wonder they were ever considered worth eating. And that's just the oyster's exterior. Once shucked, an oyster presents an organic pool of soft folds and metallic brine that has been described in terms from ribald to repulsive. Yet oysters have persevered, despite their off-putting appearance. Plucked from the water and savagely eaten while still alive, they connect us with our dormant barbarism, echoes of our Neolithic ancestors who gathered them at the water's edge.

Oysters are unbeautiful organisms, yet their taste is so compelling that they have shaped the architecture of our Chesapeake Bay environment and culture for eons. Here in the Bay's tidewater, oysters—a symbol of the opportunity for survival, for prosperity, for environmental harmony and for innovation—continue to be one of the Bay's most significant and enduring connections between our past and our present.

From the beginning, oysters have represented a central component of the Chesapeake diet. Chesapeake Paleo-Indians, in particular, consumed them in quantities so impressive that imprints of their ancient oyster feasts remain visible in the modern landscape. They're called middens—ancient trash pits of discarded shell layered over millennia like the ultimate Smith Island cake.

# INTRODUCTION

You can spot them crumbling where the waves lap at the shore, exposing piles of wafer-thin shell with every low tide. As winter set in, the Bay's native people traveled to winter camps close to the immense oyster reefs that would sustain them over the cold, dark months. Generations of Indian communities partook of the bounty, eating thousands of oysters a season. Today, these fragile middens are reminders of the long, intertwined history of Chesapeake people and oysters—remaining after most of the oyster reefs and native tribes have disappeared.

When British colonists immigrated to the Chesapeake in the seventeenth century, they were astonished by the abundance of oysters. Their diaries and letters are full of breathlessly enraptured descriptions of the Chesapeake's bounty. "Oysters there be in whole banks and beds, and those of the best. I have seen some thirteen inches long," wrote William Strachey in 1612. Coming from a land where the populace had embraced oysters as a national birthright since the time of the Romans, oysters were a colonial comfort food. In the wilderness of the New World, oysters—dislodged by hand and eaten raw with gusto—were a survival strategy.

In the several hundred years following colonization, Chesapeake residents continued to rely on the oyster reefs. Recipes from this era call for adding oysters and their liquor to a dish, cooking them until the oyster's delicate taste had been transferred and then spooning up the oysters and throwing them away. It was an embarrassment of riches—so seemingly endless was the oyster population in size and scope that it was inconceivable to the eighteenth-century Chesapeake person that humans could possibly make a dent. Oysters were so plentiful as to be disposable, so ubiquitous as to be invisible. Everyone ate them, regardless of social class, income or race.

The centrality of oysters to Bay life only grew in the nineteenth century. Due to the rapid technological advances of the Industrial Era—including steam locomotion, canning and food preservation and the newfangled practice of dredging—the slow, local harvest of oysters transformed almost overnight into an international juggernaut. Skipjacks sailed over the winter Bay, their decks piled high with the "white gold" from the bottom beds. Railroad towns like Crisfield sprang up virtually overnight on the shores of the Chesapeake, oriented toward their lifeblood, their engine—the fertile oyster reefs. From the African American women who shucked oysters in the unheated packinghouses to the powerful railroad magnates who flooded their rail lines with boxcars laden with oyster cargo, all strata of society felt the impact of the oyster boom.

# INTRODUCTION

For fifty years in the late 1800s to the turn of the century, there was no respite for the Bay's oysters. The peak of the oystering harvest was in the 1880s, when over 20 million bushels of oysters were caught each year. Even the oysters' shells were in such demand that the ancient middens along the Bay's shores were unearthed for use in lime and fertilizer.

It wasn't to last. Year by year, the oyster catch once believed to be in numbers beyond the reach of human impact dwindled. Below the water line, the reefs were now relegated to strips of productive oyster beds. By 1920, only 4 million oysters were harvested. A lower but steady harvest prevailed until the 1960s, when two virulent diseases, MSX and Dermo, devastated the remaining population and laid waste to the already-struggling wild oyster industry. Although scientific innovation has introduced a lab-created oyster capable of resisting the diseases, its potential is still being realized on newly formed oyster farms around the watershed. For wild oysters, the future is less certain. Today, the harvest hovers around 500,000 bushels or fewer of wild-caught oysters a year—a pale shadow of the oyster boom's halcyon days.

Oysters have always equaled opportunity in the Chesapeake. As we approach a watershed moment in their harvest, they now represent the possibility for change, for dialogue and for balance. Once valued only for their flavor, oysters are now championed by conservation organizations as one of the Bay's "founding fish." Oysters are touted as an environmental panacea—creating habitat, supporting the food chain and filtering the Chesapeake's formidable concentrations of sediment and algae. Watermen, too, champion oysters as one of the last Chesapeake prospects for a traditional fishing economy. For many, oysters still represent a Chesapeake where a man with a boat, a dredge and a mission can make a living for an honest day's work with his own two hands.

With the oyster population in jeopardy, watermen and environmentalists broadly agree that more Chesapeake oysters are a good thing and vitally necessary for the environment and the economy. Figuring out how to usher oysters back into the Bay is much more complicated. Do we end the oyster harvest altogether and declare a moratorium? Grow the ones for the commercial market artificially? Redouble restoration efforts while continuing with the harvesting status quo? The future of the Chesapeake's oyster population is a contentious issue, and it has pitted watermen against scientists, environmental groups against politicians.

The Chesapeake Bay and its once magnificent oyster reefs have been transformed from the verdant Eden that the first European settlers famously encountered. The water, once clear, is turbid and murky. But the oysters are still there. Though they may no longer break the waterline, oyster bars remain, gamely filtering in the face of degraded Bay. On land, oysters are stubbornly persistent in our regional culture, food and consciousness. They are an unbroken thread that connects us with the rust-stained skipjacks of the 1900s, with colonists at Jamestown and the native people of the low marshes and thick forests. Humble, simple and tasty, oysters have endured.

# Chapter 1

# THE GREAT SHELLFISH BAY

Down in the brackish depths of the Chesapeake Bay, the oysters grow. Dappled light drifts over them, stacked like three-dimensional crosswords in columns twenty feet high. The oyster reefs are enormous, yet close observation shows they are made up of small creatures: naked gobies, globules of sea squirts, clusters of barnacles. The oysters, their hosts, pull water pulled through their slitted shells and expel it again filtered and clear, plankton and sediment tidily digested. They are architects of the Bay's bottom, constructing towers of their own shells and opening up new strata to a busy community of benthic life.

Over thousands of years, *Crassostrea virginica*, the eastern oyster, flourished in the shallow, salt-infused water of the Chesapeake Bay and beyond. Ranging all along the East Coast, oyster reefs of substantial size stretched from Nova Scotia in the north to the Gulf of Mexico to the south. Small creatures and larger fish schooled through and around the oyster colonies, which seethed with aquatic animals along each link in the food chain.

The biology of the eastern oyster is relatively simple. They are filter feeders, bivalves that constantly flush water through their systems in search of the microscopic plankton drifting in the current. In the oyster's digestive process, small particles of sand or sediment are disposed of in the form of small pellets, and stripped of nutrients, a steady stream of purified water is released. In this manner, they can collectively clarify their watery atmosphere.

# CHESAPEAKE OYSTERS

Oysters require shallow water and a balance of salt to survive. The majority of the Chesapeake Bay's main stem and southern tributaries, with an average depth of twenty feet, is an ideal habitat. The Bay's ratio of saline to freshwater is also oyster-friendly. Known as "brackish," it is a tidal infusion of ocean saltwater mixed with pulses of fresher river runoff, ranging from five to thirty-five salt parts per one thousand. The Chesapeake's currents are also rich with the free-floating plankton that forms the oyster's diet. All in all, a better-suited environment for oysters than the Chesapeake Bay would be hard to find.

In the rich nursery of the Chesapeake's environment, female oysters can produce about 100 million eggs per year. Gender chameleons, they can also change sex to increase their chances of successfully spawning, from male to female and back again—an ability that, as noted oyster biologist Trevor Kinkaid once commented, "is strictly a case of Dr. Jekyll and Mrs. Hyde." Following a seasonal cycle, oysters spawn in the summer, once the water temperature has risen above sixty-eight degrees Fahrenheit. They release their eggs and sperm into the water surrounding them, broadcasting their smoky, suspended sex to the currents of fate. Once fertilized, an oyster egg becomes a free-floating larvae in about six hours and spends its first three weeks of life as a hitchhiker on the tides. This is the last time an oyster will be mobile.

Toward the end of this marine walkabout, the oyster larvae develop a foot and begin to drift toward the bottom of the water column. There, they seek a solid surface on which to permanently attach, like rocks (seldom found on the Bay's sandy bottom), hard mud or, most commonly, other oysters. Once these "spat" affix to a piling, a reed or a flat shell, they begin to grow—often facing the top of the water. Their successive growth spurts are exuded from the inside out—thin fingernails of flexible shell that harden into layers of calcified armor. In this manner, they create rusticated forms, layer upon layer of oysters growing, the shell of each forming a shelf in the water column for bristle worms, skillet fish and anemones.

Oysters in the wild grow approximately one inch per year. They can develop more rapidly in water with higher salinity and with a strong current bearing thick plankton loads. The growth and shape of individual oysters can be impacted by their position in the water column—algae at the water's sunny surface encourages swift growth, as do moderate currents that help bring the nutrients to the sessile organisms. Conversely, crowding or long tidal periods out of water can markedly slow the growing process.

An oyster's surroundings also influence its shape. Soft bottom and reefs can produce long, slender oysters, whereas hard substrate and room to expand create rounded oysters with ridged, fluted shells. And with a twenty-year life span, the eastern oyster has the capacity to grow to a hulking size; oyster fossils have been discovered that measured up to twelve inches long.

In the clear, sandy-bottomed, nutrient-flush waters of the prehistoric Chesapeake, the conditions for expansive oyster colonies were perfect. In this rich saline bath, oysters abounded; immense oyster reefs, scraping the top of the water at low tide, were one of the distinguishing landmarks of the Chesapeake Bay's ancient landscape. Their rigid masses would have billowed around the edges of the shoreline and followed the slope down into light-filled water, where silver schools of shad darted.

Above the waterline, the environment was similarly productive. Huge cypress swamps formed primordial tunnels of green above the southern Chesapeake tributaries, their knees reaching out of the water like they were contemplating rising out of the peat and roaming free. Darting through the huge stands of elm, oak, beech and chestnut were rivers of technicolor Carolina parakeets, their gaudy turquoise and acid yellow feathers striking against glossy foliage. Elk roamed the rolling hills of the upper Chesapeake, and red wolves loped in evening hunts.

Drawn to this marine and terrestrial cornucopia were populations of native people. Recent archaeological breakthroughs now suggest that Paleo-Americans were living in the Chesapeake watershed as long as thirteen thousand years ago. Their presence predates the Bay's incredible transformation after the last ice age, from Susquehanna River Valley to meandering arterial expanse, when the breaching ice melt created the waterways. These people would have known deep forests and cliffs where today there are reedy marshes and low land spreading into open water, and they would have encountered diverse populations of animals and plants that would challenge modern imaginations.

The Chesapeake Paleo-Indians were initially hunters and gatherers, and by the Late Woodland period about five thousand to three thousand years ago, their diet made the most of their fertile environment. Archaeologists have found evidence of nuts, fruits, roots, seeds, deer, black bear, squirrel, rabbit, turtles, fish, waterfowl, beaver, otter and muskrat in their dwelling sites. It was also during this period that the Chesapeake's prehistoric people began to harvest and consume substantial quantities of oysters.

The practice of harvesting wild oysters was not unique to the Chesapeake Bay in this period. Throughout the world, wherever a felicitous mix of shallow bottom and saline waters could be found, oysters flourished and people followed shortly after. In Europe and the Mediterranean, the variety was *Crassostrea edulis*, the large, flat oysters with an intense flavor profile, and *Crassostrea angulata*, the Portuguese oyster. Along the coastlines of Asia and the Pacific, oysters range from tiny and curled like squirrel's ears for the *lurida* and *sikaema* varieties to platter-sized like the hefty *gigas*. These many species were the breadcrumb trail of sustenance, indicating the presence of life-giving salt and a healthy, productive estuarine environment.

To a wandering band of nomads in a post–Ice Age world, oysters were an abundant landscape feature and a source of easy protein. Simply dislodged from their clusters, oysters could be steamed open over a fire or coaxed open with a stone tool. Regardless of where you might be on the planet, evidence of early man's heavy consumption of oysters is easy to find along any brackish waterway—oyster middens. Mixed with mussels, periwinkles, crab shells and fish bones, millions of discarded oysters shells, as fine and transparent as bone china, can be observed in the gigantic piles of dinner scraps the early peoples left behind. These ancient trash pits, formed over thousands of years, left raised, chalky scars hundreds of yards across. All around the world, oyster middens crumble at the waterline or are exposed, a white streak in the soil, by plows. Their ubiquitous presence is proof of thousands of wintry shellfish feasts, generation upon generation wading, collecting, steaming and savoring.

In the Chesapeake Bay, oysters were a seasonal winter food for the hunters and gatherers who formed communities throughout the sprawling tributary. Spawning in the summer, oysters are thin and milky, and fresh greens, berries, fish and game would have formed the bulk of a warm-weather diet. But in the winter, when thin sheets of ice formed over shorelines and forests were barren of foraging fare, oysters, now plumply inviting, would have come into season.

Middens can be found throughout the Bay's tidal reaches wherever the salinity of the water is high enough to support a healthy reef environment. These bleached oyster shell dunes cluster around snaky river oxbows, ghosts of past fishing camps used regularly year after year. For archaeologists, middens are invaluable modern tools for understanding the distant past of the Chesapeake Bay—their location, density and shape can paint a remarkably detailed picture of the Bay the Indians knew. They can also reveal troves of information about the native people themselves. In the Chesapeake, where colonists began their relentless onslaught of settlement earlier than any other location along what would be the thirteen colonies, middens are one of the few ways to understand the relationship regional people had with their environment.

Through intention or circumstance, colonists would eventually destroy, disenfranchise and displace the natives they encountered. When their populations were decimated, the only historical records of Chesapeake Indians—their oral tradition—were largely erased forever. Therefore, the earliest written accounts of the oysters in the Chesapeake come not from the native people who had harvested them for thousands of years. Instead, descriptions of oysters come from the Bay's first colonists, who documented the shellfish they saw in loving detail. Arriving four hundred years ago, filthy and bearded, the colonists were no strangers to oysters—indeed, the English were oyster enthusiasts of the highest caliber. After all, they were the product of an ancient oyster culture that had shaped their homeland for centuries.

The British Isles, with thousands of miles of gravel coastline, rich marshes and brackish estuaries, has an environment perfectly suited to nurture prodigious oyster populations. For millennia, its *Crassostrea edulis* species, like *Crassostrea virginica*, sustained bands of indigenous people who left their discarded shells behind. Britain has long been a conflicting crossroads of new peoples and cultures, and many of the waves of invaders arriving on its stony beaches have relished its copious stocks of shellfish. The Romans, in particular, had an insatiable appetite for Britain's land and resources, and their rapacious hunger extended to the rich oyster beds of the Thames, the north Kent coast and Sussex.

Romans, as the Greeks before them, were connoisseurs of the oyster's succulent delights. The Greeks had christened them "ostreum," or bones, which referred both to their shells and the subaquatic structures they created. By 400 BC, they were positioning twigs in productive oyster beds to gather and cultivate spat sets. In the third century BC, Aristotle wrote about the relocation of oysters from one bed to another to encourage plumpness and growth. The Romans embraced these practices and built on them. At Baiae and Lucrine, large oyster farms called "ostrearia" used ropes suspended by a framework of boards to produce thousands of oysters for the wealthy citizens of the realm.

Cooked or raw, Romans of all levels of society consumed great shoals of oysters. In archaeological digs at the Colosseum, oyster shells have been discovered alongside oyster pits and chicken bones—the long-forgotten remains of ancient stadium snacks. A classless food, oysters were consumed with similar gusto in debauched banquets in the Palatine Hill's marble palaces. The Emperor Vitellius alone legendarily devoured over one thousand oysters in one evening's feast. Whether this extraordinary gluttony was the result of

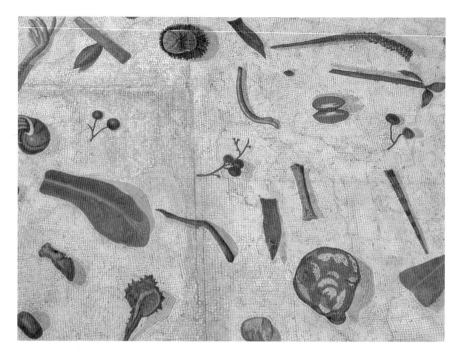

Heraclitus created "unswept room" mosaics celebrating the central role of oysters in Roman foodways in the second century BC. *Image by author.*

the oyster's fine flavor or their reputation as a potent aphrodisiac, Vitellius's appetite underscored the oyster's importance of Roman tables.

With the expansion of the Roman Empire, sources for new, exotic types of oysters were constantly being discovered and exploited, with quantities of the *edulis* delicacies sent back to the distant capital city on extensive journeys that could take weeks or even months. A quote by Mucianus indicates the extent of the Roman oyster trade: "The oysters from the Cyzicus are bigger than those from the Lucrine, gentler than those from Brittany, more flavored than those from the Medoc, spicier than those from Ephesos, more valuable than those from Illice, drier than those from Coryplas, tenderer than those from Istria, and whiter than those from Circei."

The British oyster culture, which would eventually inform English colonists who immigrated to the far shores of the New World's Chesapeake Bay, began with the arrival of Roman oyster connoisseurs in AD 43, under the rule of Emperor Claudius. Although oysters had been a minor part of the diet in the British Isles for thousands of years, their star quickly rose as the Romans invaded, conquered and fell hungrily on the vast, productive oyster reefs exposed by the dramatic tides each day. Unfortunately, the newcomers found little else on the wet, remote outpost to recommend it. "Poor Britons," commented Roman historian Sallust in AD 50, "there is some good in them after all—they produce an oyster."

"Rutupian" oysters, as the Romans referred to them, were harvested from wild stocks in the Richborough region of Kent as well as the southern coast and were consumed extensively both locally and abroad. Modern archaeologists have discovered Richborough oyster shells north and well inland at Hadrian's Wall and the Antonine Wall, evidence of transportation routes that used extensive land and water to connect to the resource. Their remnants lace Roman villa sites throughout the South of England. At an excavation at Caister-on-Sea, archaeologists stopped counting the oyster shells they uncovered once they hit the ten thousand mark.

This extraordinary, seemingly inexhaustible consumption of England's renowned shellfish would continue throughout the duration of the Roman occupation, regionally and abroad. Afterward, echoes of this molluscan golden age would reverberate through the ages, long after the Roman forts and villas were only topographical remains cloaked by a layer of turf. The British palate would, moving forward, forever have a partiality for oysters, and thanks to the technology of the invaders, the practices of oyster cultivation were now a chapter in the island's agricultural legacy.

By the late fifteenth century, when the first Britons left their families, their occupations and their familiar world behind to journey west toward a mysterious New World horizon, oysters were firmly established in the English diet. As the ships bound for the Chesapeake Bay were loaded dockside in 1607, Shakespeare had already staged *The Merry Wives of Windsor*, with its memorable line, "Why, then the world's mine oyster/ Which I with sword will open." Fittingly, recent archaeological work at the site of Globe Theatre in London also suggests that Tudor audiences may have been enjoying their own oysters as those lines were spoken. Along with crabs, periwinkles, walnuts and cherries, oysters were a common theater food in the seventeenth century.

The unassuming, ubiquitous oyster occupied a permanent, if not exalted Roman-style role in the economic and foodways traditions of England—a providential precedent in the forthcoming chapter of the British Empire. Oysters would soon transcend their role as familiar comfort food as three ships set sail toward a strange, savage land. In the Chesapeake, the humble, omnipresent oyster would transcend its role as theater food, becoming a critical method of survival for the first European settlers.

# CHAPTER 2

# A FRUITFULL AND DELIGHTSOME LAND

In a weedy space behind an office building, air-conditioning units hum away in the humidity. At a line of several ten-gallon trashcans, archaeologist Danny Schmidt casually flips the lids open to expose the oyster shells that are piled up to the lip. Palm-sized and caked with a thin film of clay, most have had the thinnest part of their shells knocked off—a sign that that they were shucked by someone in a hurry to get to the contents inside. Danny reaches in and sifts through the top layer of shells. "We have eighty thousand of them in here," he remarks. "They're all still in pretty good shape—for being four hundred years old."

They are. Other than some broken edges and a crust of mud from enterprising wasps, these oyster shells look remarkably like anything you might find paving a local driveway. It makes sense when you consider that they spent the last four centuries deep inside an abandoned well at the site of the Jamestown colony. Discarded along with an incredible assortment of period trash from broken crockery to crucibles, these eighty thousand hurriedly shucked oysters were one part of the survival strategy for the hapless souls who attempted to settle on the James River.

Struggling to eke out a new life in a wildly foreign environment, the Jamestown colonists stuck to foods they could identify. The oyster, a staple of English fare, was a taste of home that did not need to be cultivated, hunted or even cooked. Plucked free and eaten raw in their own shells, these oysters were often the only certain meal after Jamestown's crops had failed and disease ravaged the settlement as Indians circled in the underbrush, just hidden from view.

Unlike the hardy Pilgrims, the Jamestown settlers were capitalists, in search of the riches or land the New World would doubtlessly provide. Tradesmen and gentlemen, fishmongers, barrel makers, musicians and the pampered second sons of English gentry, the Jamestown colonists represented all trades and levels of society. Despite signing up for the ultimate Chesapeake colonial experience, most had almost no basic survival skills, and few even knew how to use a firearm. Despite this, all 105 were united in their willingness to gamble everything familiar in the hope for a better life.

The Jamestown Colony had significant backers and was underwritten by a corporation called the Virginia Company. Support for the settlement was raised through lotteries, and 1,700 shareholders were cultivated through pamphlets, broadsides, sermons and plays—the Jacobean equivalent of a marketing blitz. Each shareholder—called, brilliantly for the armchair tourist crowd, "adventurers"—contributed twelve pounds, ten shillings toward the cost of outfitting the colony, with promises of great returns on their investment if the successes of the East India Company or Muscovy Company were any example.[1]

It was a risky venture. Several earlier English attempts to colonize the region had failed, losing money, costly supplies and the lives of hundreds of settlers. The most infamous was the Roanoke Colony. In 1584, 1585 and 1587, Sir Walter Raleigh, the influential, staggeringly wealthy favorite of Queen Elizabeth, underwrote several settlements. Each was on the coast of modern-day North Carolina, just below the confluence of the Chesapeake Bay and the ocean. Despite the clear abundance of the landscape, two main problems—bungled relations with the native tribes and the constant specter of starvation—stymied the attempts at settlement in dramatic fashion. So utter was Roanoke's collapse that a later rescue mission found nothing left of the 1587 settlement other than a few cryptic words scratched into a nearby tree. Yet in an example of early spin doctoring, the reports from the collapsed colonies gave no hint of the troubles that future colonists might face in the Chesapeake region. Rather, the Roanoke accounts were so enticing that enormous amounts of capital continued to be raised for ships, manpower and colonial recruitment efforts.

In statements written by Roanoke scientist and explorer Thomas Harriot, all manner of natural resources from "oyle and furres" to "beastes and foules" were described in exhaustive and calculating detail. Harriot's observations extended to "the nature and manners of the people of the countrey," whom he described as "very handsome, and goodly people, and in their behavior as mannerly, and civil, as any of Europe."[2] A series of sensitive, highly detailed watercolor paintings and maps by artist John White captured the local flora, fauna and regional tribes, providing rich visual context. By Harriot's accounts, the mouth of the Chesapeake was an amazingly productive environment, full of mysterious plants and animals. Not all were unfamiliar, however. Harriot described huge shoals of oysters flourishing in the shallow coves ringing the barrier islands: "Oisters, some very great, and some small, some round, and some of a long shape: they are found both in salt water and brackish, and those that we had out of salt water are far better then the other as in our countrey."

The oyster reefs, though recognizable to Harriot, were of a size not seen in England since Roman times. He wrote, "Of oyster shels there is plentie ynough: for besides diuers other particular places where are abundance, there is one shallowe sounde along the coast, where for the space of many miles together in length, & two or three miles in breadth, the ground is nothing els, being but halfe a foote or a foote vnder water for the most part."

These oyster shells, Harriot knew, represented not only an easily harvested food source but also a vital building material. Oyster shells, once charred over a fire, could be used to make lime, an essential component to bricklaying and masonry. Doubtless his report was tailored to encourage English dreams of great, civilized brick towns in the New World, whose handsome buildings would all be cemented with oyster shell mortar.

Ultimately published several years later in Harriot's *A Briefe and True Report of the New Found Land of Virginia*, these reports would inform the European public's perceptions of the New World. Even today they comprise one of the richest troves documenting the Algonquian culture and early mid-Atlantic coastal environment at the time of first contact. When published, Harriot's Roanoke journals were a sensation. They were widely read, and their descriptions of an otherworldly environment exposed Elizabethan audiences to the period equivalent of a lunar landing. *A Briefe and True Report* also served as a sort of guide for would-be settlers. But Harriot's decidedly optimistic text—mostly propaganda—omitted the repercussions of deep troubles caused by the settler's nonexistent survival skills and a deep dependence on local tribes for food. Ironically, Harriot's text was not published until 1588—the same year then-governor John White returned to Roanoke and discovered the 115 settlers missing and the colony abandoned. Blithely unaware, future settlers would be destined to repeat the mistakes of

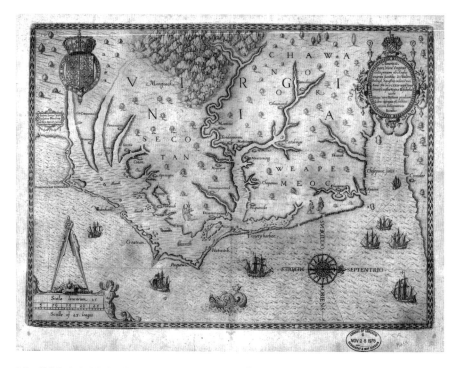

John White's 1590 detailed map of Roanoke depicts oyster shoals and the mouth of the Chesapeake Bay. Copy by Theodor de Bry. *Library of Congress Collections*.

Roanoke as England intensified its colonial efforts along the oyster-rich coast of the Mid-Atlantic.

Despite Roanoke's spectacular collapse, British investors were undeterred. With great risk comes great reward, and there was plenty of financial incentive for European investors to continue sending settlers to the Chesapeake. In the Virginia Company's vision, the New World north of the Caribbean was just an outline on a map, an unknown quantity whose hidden interior might well contain a route to China's spices, tea, silk and porcelain. In addition to scouting for the fabled Northwest Passage, a colony could be a source of raw materials—lumber, minerals, furs—and would secure a foothold in Europe's race for colonial fortunes. In "Ode to the Virginia Voyage," written by a friend of a Virginia Company investor, the lofty expectations for the enterprise are clear: "And cheerfully at sea/ success you still entice/ To get the pearl and gold, and ours to hold/ Virginia, Earth's only paradise!"

The ambitious undertaking was blessed by the newly crowned King James, who saw an opportunity to advance England's lagging position in Europe's New World land grab with little cost to the country. But the speculation at

Jamestown would indeed come at a dear price. Its outcomes were, at least initially, anything but the richly dyed silks at the end of a Northwest Passage. Instead, the hapless colonists met with every misfortune: disease, murder, starvation, incompetence, aggression and, in a turn of deep desperation, even cannibalism.

Given the less-than-heroic beginnings of Jamestown's history, it is hardly any surprise that Plymouth's origin story is the American favorite. Jamestown's early years, though morbidly compelling, are difficult to use as a patriotic rallying cry. Even Virginia, where Jamestown has long been touted as the true first colony, has struggled to come to terms with its own past. In 1957, believing that the original site had long washed away into the James River, the state set about creating a tidy theme park celebrating the hardscrabble colony. Wattle-and-daub structures connected by paved paths took visitors on a quaint, rose-colored stroll through the past. Populated by costumed interpreters, Jamestown was presented as a charming village full of industrious settlers who were happy to demonstrate their matchlock muskets or doff their metal helmets for a quick try-on. Visitors could try their hand at ninepins, explore a replica of an Indian village and enjoy an educational, diverting trip to the past where Jamestown seemed tidy, productive and safe.

While Jamestown Settlement, the park, was doing a profitable business in friendly living history and colonial patriotism, the real Jamestown, not a mile away, was quietly entombed in red clay. Not eroded away at all, the colony's remains clung stubbornly to the original point where it had been so ill-advisedly established four hundred years ago. In the meantime, the site had been well used by different generations who had braved the wetlands and biting flies to make their mark on the island. Jamestown's cache, buried deep, remained remarkably undisturbed.

In 1994, with statewide commemorative event planning underway for the 400th anniversary of the fort's establishment, Preservation Virginia charged archaeologist Bill Kelso with finding what remained—or didn't—of the original fort. Kelso, an expert in Virginia archaeology who had previously worked as the head of archaeology at Monticello, began work armed with period accounts and a crude 1608 map of the region. Digging only a stone's throw from the water's edge, he hit artifacts almost immediately—pins, doublet buttons, copper pieces and oyster shells—scores of them. Postholes surfaced, their stains on the soil like a connect-the-dots puzzle.

The project attracted local support, along with a team of archaeologists. Pitching in on the project was a local kid, Danny Schmidt, who arrived one day to volunteer and never left. He has since spent over twenty-five years

Archaeologist Danny Schmidt and Jamestown's collection of oyster shells. *Image by author.*

working at the site. Leaving to attend college, he returned every summer and stayed on after graduation as a staff archaeologist, continuing chipping away at the layers of earth covering Jamestown's past.

Schmidt still conveys a boyish exuberance during his occasional tours of the site, his professional demeanor slipping to reveal a kid who just wanted to find cool stuff in the ground. And it is with this same "hey, look what I found" excitement that he shows the prizes of Jamestown's enormous collections on behind-the-scenes tours—including the rows of oysters in trashcans, lined up behind the collections building of the archaeological site like Pandora's boxes. The dig continues today—and with every spadeful of clay soil mixed with wafers of oyster shell, the recreated Jamestown's comfortable rosy glow dims and the harrowing experience of Jamestown's settlers is exhumed.

Like Roanoke, Jamestown's success and failure hinged on two major, intertwined issues: food and Indian relations. Yet the Virginia Company did not learn from Roanoke's cautionary tale. Rather, the Jamestown settlers were encouraged to rely yet again upon local native people for food. Indeed, detailed instructions sent over with the settlers to be opened upon arrival plainly stated that the trading with natives for food should begin immediately, "not being sure how your own seed corn will prosper in the first year." Like preceding settlements, Jamestown would teeter on the thin lip between survival and imminent disaster.

On April 26, 1607, after a three-month route from England via the Canaries and the West Indies, the *Susan Constant,* the *Godspeed* and the *Discovery* entered the Chesapeake Bay. Dropping anchor near a spot they named Cape Henry after a son of King James, the settlers sent out groups to scout. Lead by experienced explorer Christopher Newport, the men spent the day exploring but, according to George Percy, a member of the group, found "nothing worth the speaking of, but faire meddowes and goodly tall Trees."

Hiking eight miles inland the next day, the scouting expedition encountered a group of native men clustered around a fire. Startled, the men scattered from their hearth, hastily abandoning their dinner in the process. As the Englishmen drew near, they saw oysters—a familiar sight—roasting over the fire. Their reaction would foreshadow the struggles with Indians that would haunt the colonists for the next decade. Without hesitation, the hungry men fell on the steaming oysters. According to one man in the scouting party, the filched oysters were "very large and delicate in taste."

The next few weeks found the settlers journeying farther north, following a wide river they named after King James several miles into the interior of the new country. It was a place of remarkable resources, in concentrations unknown to the English. "Having also at the mouth of every brook and in every creek both store and exceeding good fish of divers kinds," Christopher Newport wrote, "in ye large sounds neere the sea are multitudes of fish, banks of oysters." John Smith concurred, waxing poetic that "Heaven & earth never agreed better to frame a place for man's habitation…Here are mountaines, hils, plaines, valleyes, rivers, and brookes, all running most pleasantly into a faire Bay, compassed but for the mouth, with fruitfull and delightsome land."[3]

The landscape, though wild, was plainly inhabited. As the ships followed the James River away from the Chesapeake's main stem, there were several more or less peaceful interactions with groups of local Indians. Though the English thought better than to re-create what they perceived as the barbaric behavior of the Spanish and Portuguese in the Caribbean, they were motivated more by a vague sense of their own superiority than any notion of equality. "Have Great Care not to Offend the naturals if You Can Eschew it," the Virginia Company had advised, continuing, "and how Weary Soever your Soldiers be Let them never trust the Country people with the Carriage of their Weapons, for if they Run from You with Your Shott which they only fear, they will Easily kill them all with their arrows."

Overly confident after a few peaceful interactions, the colonists paid little attention to the Virginia Company's cautious counsel. To the English, the "naturals" were childlike and primitive, regarded with an air of fascination but entertained with cheap trinkets—hardly people to be feared. Though the colony's backers were emphatic that tribal villages should be given a wide berth when a settlement location was determined, the well-intended advice was also ignored. "You must take Especial Care that you Choose a Seat for habitation that Shall not be over burthened with Woods near your town…that it may Serve for a Covert for Your Enimies round about You," the colony's directives plainly stated.

Yet over the next few weeks, a location for the fort was chosen that directly contradicted the Virginia Company's directions: a marshy peninsula, not far downriver from nearby Native American towns and villages. The appointed colony president, Edward-Maria Wingfield, also deemed it unnecessary to ready any the fledgling settlement's defenses. Wingfield was highborn—which, along with some limited military experience, was the most important criteria for his appointment as president—but completely inexperienced in any of life's practicalities. Accustomed to an easy life of comfort, Wingfield's dulled survival instincts perceived no threat in the local tribes.

As fate would have it, Wingfield's foolish decision almost immediately backfired. While several of the most capable soldiers were away on an exploratory trip down the river, hundreds of native warriors attacked the defenseless encampment. Only the booms of cannon fire from one of the nearby ships startled the attackers enough to stanch the flow of arrows. More than a dozen men were wounded.

Wingfield belatedly organized a palisade to be erected around the camp. Over the next few months, the colonists would hear the unmistakable thwack of arrow against wood during intermittent attacks many times. One colonist "going out to doe natural necessity" beyond the wall's protection was picked off by an arrow to the head.

The fort's inadequate security was not the only serious problem. While initially all hands had fallen to the work of clearing trees and sowing crops in a flurry of teamwork, very quickly, the societal hierarchies deeply ingrained in English culture had begun to surface. Idleness soon prevailed among the better sort.

The lower-born settlers became the workhorses, attempting to scratch fields and fences from the low-lying island. Their odds for success were low as the number of helping hands dwindled by the day. Despite an early flurry of enthusiastic pitching in, the higher-born colonists quickly exhausted their interest in the endless drudgery of colony creation. Even after the ships and their crew returned to England, taking much of the able bodies with them, the titled settlers ignored the trees that needed felling and the corn shoots that snarled with weeds. Many of the colonists still lived in tents. Four hundred years later, Kelso and his crew unearthed carved ivory dice the size of sugar cubes—testament to just how Jamestown's better sort wiled away the humid July.

John Smith would later recall of that summer, "At this time our diet was for the most part water and bran, and three ounces of little better stuffe in bread for five men a meale, and thus we lived neere three months: our lodgings under the boughs of trees, the savages being our enemies, whom we neither knew or understood; occasion I thinke sufficient to make men sicke and die."[4]

A man of military training with practical experience as a hired mercenary, John Smith was far more knowledgeable than most of the other colonists in matters of survival, exploration and the art of diplomacy. As the summer ground on and the situation became dire, he was vaulted into a leadership role. Smith's frank assessment was astute—within a few weeks, disease and starvation would halve the settlement's population.

The low-lying, marshy conditions of Jamestown Island began to take their toll on the settlers, as did the colony's reliance on river water for drinking.

Mosquitoes plagued the men incessantly, and those not afflicted by symptoms of malaria were sickened by the increasingly brackish water, which grew saltier as the summer's drought progressed. One colonist's journal reported the grim repercussions in a laundry list of macabre fatalities:

> *The sixt of August there died John Asbie of the bloudie flixe. The ninth day died George Flowre of the swelling. The tenth day died William Bruster gentleman, of a wound given by the savages and was buried the eleventh day…Our men were destroyed with cruell diseases such as the swellings, flixes, burning fevers, and by warres, but for the most part they died of meere famine…every night and day, for the space of six weeks, some departing out of the World, many times three or four in a night; in the morning, their bodies trailed out of their Cabins like Dogs to be buried.*[5]

Too sick to forage for food or tend the fields, the weakened settlers perished one after another. It was ironic. Surrounded by some of the most productive estuarine environments known to man, the settlers were starving. George Percy had earlier described the bounty to be had in rapturous terms: "We got good store of Mussels and Oysters, which lay on the ground as thick as stones. We opened some, and found in many of them Pearls… this Country is a fruitful soil, bearing many goodly and fruitful Trees, as Mulberries, Cherries, Walnuts…in great abundance."[6]

Now, with the surviving men unable to stir from their sickbeds to gather this plenty, Smith knew that Jamestown must trade with the local tribes if they wanted to make it through the winter. As a hired soldier with a good ear for languages, he had traveled across Europe and Turkey, managing to make himself understood with a pidgin mix of English and local dialects. This would come in handy as he navigated trade with the Chickahominy, Paspahegh and Pamunkey—tribes who tended to address the English with a mixture of contempt and aggression tempered with intermittent shows of goodwill.

Smith's ability to communicate was an important asset, but the tenor of his approach with the local tribes was just as critical. In his years of martial self-education, he'd read up on his Machiavelli and had taken to heart the idea of the worthy adversary. Smith strategized that a healthy respect for the "salvages" would lead to productive parley and a steady supply of food. His early attempts were fruitful. He spread out his trade network throughout several villages, "lest they perceived my too great want" and sense weakness. He returned to Jamestown laden with oysters, corn, fish and venison.

John Smith's trade journeys and exploratory missions would lead him and a small crew in small, bathtub-shaped vessel called a shallop along many of the Chesapeake's waterways. Each foray was an exercise in Smith's unique brand of diplomacy: respect comingled with suspicion, intimidation and not a small amount of showmanship. Smith's approach was not always successful. Most famously, Smith was held in captivity for several months by a chief, Powhatan, and his brother, Opechancanough, after exploratory trade mission on the Chicahominy went awry. Smith was headed for execution, but Powhatan's daughter, Pocahontas, interceded on Smith's behalf and abruptly defused the situation. It was the stuff that launched a million legends and just as many improbable romantic tales, but more than likely, Smith's survival hung mostly on luck and his peculiar style of gravitas. It was an ordeal that could have easily turned for the worse. During the same trip, another member of Smith's crew, George Cassen, was cut to pieces with mussel shells, disemboweled and burned at the stake by Opechancanough's men.[7]

Several times, the colony came near to collapse in John Smith's absence, first in January 1608 when Smith returned to find colonists still living in tents and holes in the ground. One settler later described their lot as "at the point of death, utterly destitute of all houses." Even when living conditions improved under Smith's leadership, the colonists seemed unable to trade or even forage without direct oversight. "Though there be fish in the sea, fowls in the air, and beasts in the woods, their bounds are so large, they so wilde, and we so weake and ignorant, we cannot much trouble them," Smith wrote. Returning from another exploratory mission, Smith discovered that colonists were incapable of monitoring the little rations they had: "In searching our casked corne, wee found it helfe rottern, the rest so consumed with the many thousand rats that we knewe not how to keepe that little wee had…This did drive us all to our wits end."[8]

Smith had little patience for what he saw as lack of initiative and immediately set about enforcing a shape up or ship out regime. His first task was to clean house. Of Jamestown's layabout gentlemen, Smith proposed a rule certain to rouse them from their dice games: "He who shall not work shall not eat." Smith also took a pragmatic approach to the problem of having a concentrated population surviving off a limited amount of food. He divided the group up into three parts and sent one to live with a friendly local tribe in exchange for copper. Two smaller groups were dispersed to widely spaced locations so that they might forage without competition.

One of the groups was sent south, closer to the salty mouth of the James River. There, oyster shoals crowded the riverbanks and reliable sustenance could be plucked from the waterline. A diet of mostly shellfish for nine weeks did take a toll, even if the settlers managed to all survive. One of the group later complained (perhaps justifiably): "This kind of feeding caused all our skin to peel off from head to foot as though we had been dead." Smith took no notice of these grumbles. Under his leadership, he urged regular downriver forays to the "the Shells which wee must goe or starve."[9]

Under Smith's leadership, twenty new houses were built, corn was planted with the guidance of a few local native people and brisk trade resumed with the nearby tribes. By July, when the next resupply ship arrived, the few settlers still living in Jamestown were healthy and had made good headway on critical projects for winter survival. For the briefest moment, all was well. Perhaps it could have stayed so. Had the Virginia Company not decided to infuse the barely righted colony with so many more mouths to feed, things might have been different. Behind the resupply ship, Smith learned, were eight more vessels laden with hundreds of new colonists. He also heard that one of the ships carried a new charter drafted by the Virginia Company that would strip the lowborn Smith of the presidency and install a suitably titled leader. Smith's days were numbered—and as they dwindled, so did Jamestown's hopes for stability.

Shortly after the arrival of several hundred new colonists, John Smith abruptly departed for England. Returning from negotiations with an upriver village, a bag of gunpowder exploded in his lap onboard the boat in a freak accident. An eyewitness reported that the blast "tore the flesh from his body and thighs, nine of ten inches square in the most pitifull manner; but to quench the tormenting fire he leaped over-boord into the deepe river."[10] With no doctor at the colony to treat his injuries, he was forced to leave on the first ship bound for London to have his wounds tended.

Smith would ultimately survive, but his injuries would leave him childless. His legacy was not destined to carry on in his lineage. Instead, Smith found lasting fame in the writings he published about his Jamestown experiences and in an incredible, highly detailed map of the region compiled during his Chesapeake expeditions. His stories informed perceptions of the New World—its native people and their customs, the environment's florid abundance. Used together, they became a settler's guide to the Bay and its tributaries, guiding generations of Bay-bound Europeans.

However, that was years in the future. Jamestown was now teeming with a fresh population of starry-eyed settlers, seemingly eager to make the same mistakes as their predecessors. The same problems continued to plague the venture—idleness, side projects, inept diplomacy and the

John Smith's 1608 map of the Chesapeake Bay. *Library of Congress Collections.*

mistaken belief that more food was always forthcoming from trade or resupply. This time, Smith would not be there to save them with his practical solutions.

Danny Schmidt and the Jamestown archaeology team have only recently excavated the layers of soil containing evidence of the next wretched chapter in the settlement's history. The rough outlines of a cellar, filled in and covered over during the summer following the "Starving Time" of 1609 –10, would prove to be a time capsule. Perfectly preserving the undisturbed remains of that miserable year, its contents bore macabre testament to the suffering endured by the settlers after Smith's departure.

As the dig began in 2012, the cellar's clay-caked contents seemed routine: broken crockery, copper scraps and pipe fragments. Then an unusual item, turtle shells, began to appear in the common household trash. These were stinkpots or musk turtles, tiny creatures capable of producing a powerful stench.[11] Apparently, as the food stores dwindled, the colonists started getting creative about the kinds of species they would consider eating. "They're foraging for anything they can get their hands on. We find loads of turtle shells," Schmidt explained. "One of the colonists, William Strachey, later wrote that some people were eating a turtle a day."

As Schmidt and the other archaeologists continued to dig, even more exotic remains emerged from the excavation site. Bones of crows, cormorants, bottle nose dolphin, venomous snakes, dogs, cats and horses were all found intermingled with broken dishes and bits of charcoal. The fragments were indications of the settlement's worsening conditions, as the colonists were compelled to eat species normally considered unpalatable or taboo. Stirrups were found among the discards, too. Once the horses were consumed, there was no need for the saddles to ride them.

"Then haveinge fedd upon our horses and other beastes as longe as they Lasted," wrote George Percy in his descriptions of the Starving Time. "We weare gladd to make shifte with vermin as doggs Catts, Ratts and myce…all was fishe thatt Came to Nett to satisfye Crewell hunger, as to eate Bootes shoes or any other leather some Colde come by."[12]

As the team used trowels and brushes to gently displace soil, they uncovered even more bones. Brittle teeth and skull fragments were exposed to sunlight for the first time in four hundred years. These were, by far, the most taboo bones of all. Cut marks scraped into their surfaces indicated butchery. Forensic anthropologists at the Smithsonian would later confirm what the Jamestown archaeologists' suspected. When there was nothing else left to eat, the colonists started to cannibalize their dead.

The skull belonged to a fourteen-year-old girl, whose brain, tongue, cheeks and leg muscles were eaten by fellow colonists, probably not long after her death.[13] Horrible, certainly, but at least she died of starvation first. Not all Jamestown's cannibalism victims got that courtesy. George Percy's diaries described the trial and execution of a man who confessed (after being hanged by his thumbs) to killing, salting and consuming his pregnant wife. He was burned alive at the stake in punishment—not a routine method of execution, but perhaps fitting, given the horror of the crime. Percy's accounts suggested that the public execution might not have been enough to deter others from similar behavior: "And now famin beginneinge to Looke gastely and pale in every face, thatt notheinge was Spared to mainteyne Lyfe and to doe those things which seame incredible, as to digge upp deade corpes outt of graves and to eate them. And some have Licked upp the Bloode which hathe fallen from their weake fellowes."[14]

By March 1610, only fifty colonists remained of the five hundred who had filled the settlement at Smith's departure, six months before. It would be another two months before a ship arrived to relieve the remaining souls. That

Modern crosses mark the many graves of Jamestown's doomed settlers. *Image by author.*

vessel carried survivors from the *Sea Venture*, part of a 1609 resupply fleet that had blown off course in a hurricane and was shipwrecked in Bermuda—a tale that would later inspire Shakespeare's *The Tempest*. It had taken nine months for two new ships to be created from Bermuda's cedar wood and for the members of the shipwreck to set sail for Virginia.

What the colonists from the *Sea Venture* shipwreck were about to witness surely made many long for their forsaken Carribbean paradise. Arriving at the mouth of the James River, the ship stopped at one of the smaller Chesapeake outposts, Point Comfort. There, they met George Percy, who, in an act of cowardly self-preservation, had fled Jamestown. Apparently Percy warned them of the conditions upriver at the settlement, for the captain stopped on the sail to Jamestown at the oyster reefs that had sustained the small group at Smith's command the winter before. There, they loaded up on thousands of oysters, gathering as many as they could carry.[15]

Upon arrival in Jamestown, the colony seemed deserted—dirt paths bare, crude huts with tiny glassless windows like black eyes. The *Sea Venture*'s captain ordered the church bell rung, to rouse any people still remaining. As the bell tolled, the handful of Jamestown colonists staggered out, according to Percy, "lamentable to behowlde them for many throwe extreme hunger have Runne outt of their naked bedds being so Leane that they Looked Lyke Anotamies Cryeinge owtt we are starved."[16] Those oysters, it seemed, would come in handy after all.

As Danny Schmidt leads the way to the grassy area behind the modern Historic Jamestown collections storage, the oppressive humidity and persistent biting flies give a brief glimpse into the particular miseries offered by Jamestown Island. On that day, high tides had encouraged the marsh water to creep up the manicured lawn. Just off the path, a snapping turtle the size of a hubcap trundled gracelessly in the momentarily reclaimed swamp. "There's so many of these oyster shells we can't store them all inside," Schmidt calls over his shoulder as he leads the way to the row of trashcans. "Eighty thousand of anything takes up a lot of space."

The oyster shells he displays were uncovered in the 2012 dig. Like a layer of scalloped icing, they skimmed above the silent sorrows buried below. The oyster shells were the last addition to the cellar before it was sealed up forever, and the first thing Kelso, Schmidt and the other archaeologists found as they went looking for the Starving Time. To a casual onlooker, they are not immediately evocative on first sight—indeed, they have little to distinguish them from modern examples dredged up from the mouth of the James River. But this oyster midden, contained in trashcans, represents a cornerstone of Jamestown's salvation.

The arrival of the *Sea Venture* and its supplies marked a watershed moment for the imperiled settlement. These river oysters, shucked quickly and eaten on the shell, provided sustenance for a community that otherwise would have been just more bones layered on the ones buried before. Without them, perhaps Plymouth would truly have deserved its claim to fame as the "first colony." Instead, with bellies stretched full over dozens of oysters, Jamestown's colonists and the hundreds of thousands to follow kept arriving on the Chesapeake's beaches. Oysters would provide a literal and figurative foundation for the Bay's hardscrabble settlers. Their houses were held together by oyster shell mortar, and their bodies were fueled with the easy protein of a familiar touchstone in the wilderness—oysters, in numbers beyond counting, thickly encrusting the shores of the Chesapeake's many-fingered tributaries.

# CHAPTER 3

# A COLONY OYSTERS BUILT

In the next hundred years following Jamestown's ill-fated founding, the Chesapeake proved to be a popular destination for European immigrants—many of them indentured servants—bound to the New World. Seeking fresh opportunity for land, wealth and status, these colonists had little notion of what was in store for them on the other side of the Atlantic Ocean. The Chesapeake of the colonial period was a far cry from the paradise promoted by investors back in England—it was the frontier.

Tobacco, a fad of the most ubiquitous sort in Europe, was the all-persuasive immigration incentive for seventeenth-century settlers. All levels of society and ages smoked what King James excoriated as a "filthie noveltie" and a "stinking black fume."[17] There was a staggering amount of money to be made in meeting the ever-growing demand. Orinoco tobacco, a sweetly scented strain from Trinidad, did well in the hot, intensely humid climate of the Chesapeake. This was fortunate, since land, at least in the eyes of the British, was cheap, arable and for the taking, and the Chesapeake's unique watershed topography allowed for almost limitless access.

The Bay's clear tributaries reached deep into the land's interior, forming watery highways that made travel easy and fast for local canoes and international trade ships alike. Within a few decades, tobacco plantations proliferated along Chesapeake rivers, radiating from the initial epicenter of Jamestown and spreading along the Bay's southernmost tributaries. The names given these properties speak volumes about the mentality of the settlers who established them. Called "Neglect," "Folly" or "Despair"—one truly wretched soul even named his property "Cuckhold's Hope"—they convey the sense that perhaps the gamble on tobacco wasn't worth it, after all.

Yet the number of plantations and planters only continued to increase as time progressed. In Maryland, for example, the number of settlers grew from barely 200 in 1645 to 3,700 in 1665—a population growth of 1,500 percent in only twenty years.[18] Due to malaria and sometimes just drudgery, most of these Chesapeake colonists wouldn't see their forty-fifth birthday. Their grim, squalid lives, intensely focused on work and filling their bellies, left little behind of substance and even less on paper. To get a clearer picture of early Chesapeake colonial life, you have to dig—literally.

Jane Cox has spent countless hours sifting through the trash, houses and graves of early Chesapeake colonists. A Cultural Resources Planner with Maryland's Anne Arundel County government, Cox is an archaeologist with a bent toward historic preservation. Unlike other archaeologists, who might rescue sites for posterity or restoration, Cox gleans what she can from the foundations of seventeenth-century houses or colonial cellars before they are transformed under tidy suburban lawns and cul-de-sacs.

Much of Cox's work is done outside the charmingly crooked colonial streets of Annapolis. Though it has been the state capital since 1694, town formation in the Chesapeake, with its convenient waterways, lagged throughout the late seventeenth and early eighteenth century and Annapolis was no exception. For the Bay's population, it simply wasn't necessary. Goods, services and resources all came on the tide, something that encouraged self-sufficiency at a level unknown in other British colonies. In 1678, Lord Baltimore described the dispersed population: "We have none That are called or cann be called Townes. In most places there are not fifty houses in the space of Thirty Myles." Even St. Mary's City, Maryland's first capital city, was said by Lord Baltimore to "hardly be call'd a Towne."[19]

Over a pint, Cox explains this uniquely Chesapeake rejection of colonial town creation.

*In the early eighteenth century, Annapolis is a backwater. Nobody bothers to come here. The government is trying to do everything they can to convince people this is a population center that they need to spend a lot of time in, but they don't need it. There's no need for that kind of centralized place. What pops up throughout the region archaeologically is these larger plantations developing as city centers with all these resources and suppliers and craftsmen developing around them…and almost every single one of them had beautiful access to the waterfront. Essentially their own mini-ports.*

Many of these sites are now marinas or waterfront estates or businesses. Unlike downtown Annapolis, where the remaining eighteenth-century buildings are clear guideposts to modern-day archaeologists, nothing much remains of the bygone plantations of the seventeenth and eighteenth centuries. In fact, Cox and her colleagues would have little notion of where to start excavating on these riverside sites, if not for the clues that make their way out of the soil with every hard rain. Gleaming oyster shell fragments poke out of the ground—Cox's breadcrumb trail to follow to the Chesapeake's colonial period.

Oysters, just as they had been for the Bay's native people and the earliest settlers, continued to be an essential element of Chesapeake life as the years progressed. "Civilizing" the landscape to European standards meant clearing fields for farming and pastures for livestock—creating ample sources of food on the hoof or in the soil. Rather than foraging, by the late seventeenth century, the colonists were eating more things their British counterparts would have recognized, like beef, pork and grains. They had a penchant for familiar food and even more for resources that were easily accessed. Oysters, being both, remained a vitally important resource even as the colonial reliance on other wild harvests and game waned. For most of the Chesapeake's population, closely hugging the waterways, oysters remained a cornerstone of the daily meal. A Virginia colonist in 1623 wrote baldly, "The most evident hope from altogether starving is oysters." Even as other options became available, oysters remained integral to the Chesapeake way of life.

Court records from Maryland in March 15, 1663, suggest the extreme importance of oysters as a survival food for early colonists. A sailor named Tobias Dunkin arrived at the tobacco plantation of William Bromall in 1662 to pick up some tobacco, assisted by a fellow sailor. In the plantation's water access, along a cove, a canoe had been stowed full of oysters. Dunkin helped himself to a few before being confronted by the furious plantation owner, who, in the words of the other sailor, "rayled att us, asking of us what wee did doe there?" The sailor replied, "that wee were eating a few Oysters, Telling him wthall, Hee need not bee soe angry for eating a few oysters, for they cost him nothing." Bromall was not mollified. He argued with the sailors that "they cost him his labour, for that hee had beene all the day in getting of them." Even when the sailors assured him they would pay for the oysters they had eaten, Bromall was so irate he swore at the two men, "damme mee you Dogges I will kill you, If there bee noe more Sea Dogges in the world!" He then fired his gun among the sailors, wounding several, and set his dogs on the rest.[20] Bromall's actions, teetering on the edge of insanity, indicate the value of a boat full of oysters—free, but also priceless. The thin white line between starvation and survival for Chesapeake planters, they were worth fighting for.

For archaeologists like Jane Cox, this vital interconnectedness between the Chesapeake's landscape and its people can be read in the huge deposits of discarded oyster shells found at every colonial location. "No matter how poor or how wealthy you were, you had direct access to the water," states Cox. "Based on the archaeological record, all those people were partaking of oysters. It's in every archaeological collection, representing of a large part of their diet. They were all pulling oysters from their immediate environment. Oysters are so thick at this point, up every river, it's almost like somebody would have their corn on one side of their house, and then they'd go out on the dock and go sort out their oysters for dinner on the other side."

Like the oyster middens of the Chesapeake's Indians, archaeologists studying the colonial period find rich troves of information buried in the oyster trash piles of the seventeenth and eighteenth centuries. The shells tell volumes about how often people ate oysters and in what settings, but they can also convey information about daily life—in particular, the high tolerance of colonists for strong smells and living in proximity to their own waste. In an era before curbside pickup, one's trash pit was wherever it was most convenient—directly outside the main entrance to the home, or in a disused cellar under your living quarters. "Yes," says Cox matter-of-factly, "They are living on top of their trash. The cellars that we see are filled in over a surprisingly long time period. When you no longer need that sub-floor storage, that's when it starts getting filled in. Imagine—rotting oyster shells under the floorboards! We find tons of rodent bones, too—it must have been disgusting!"

Backfilled colonial cellars are time capsules. The oyster shells are found comingled with all the sorts of household goods you might scrape off a plate after dinner: broken plates, animal bones, crab claws, bent metal pieces and fractured tobacco pipes. Layered densely like packing peanuts, they provide protection to the artifacts buried with them, taking decades, sometimes centuries to break down. But not all of Cox's findings have been as innocuous as ancient kitchen scraps. While excavating a 1660s-era cellar on a property called Leavy Neck, she discovered how broadly some colonists defined the meaning of "trash." She said, "We start excavating, and it looks like the ten other cellars we had dug. Oh, there's an animal bone, oh, here's an antler, here's a pocket of utilitarian ceramics, here's a bucket of oyster shells. We keep going down, maybe a foot, and that's when we saw the human head."

What Cox and her team had discovered in 1991 was the body of a boy, an indentured servant who had spent the last three hundred years in a shallow grave lined with household garbage and oyster shells. The teenager had been quite literally stuffed, with the aid of a milk pan, into a hastily dug depression in the cellar and then covered up with trash. From the newer layers of trash in the cellar covering the grave site, it was obvious that the family continued living, perhaps for years, above their little secret.

The story told by the Leavy Neck cellar's oyster shells and their macabre contents shines a light on another gritty aspect of life in the colonial Chesapeake: indentured servitude. Scholars estimate that between 70 and 80 percent of settlers in the seventeenth-century Chesapeake arrived as indentured servants.[21] Fulfilling the demand for cheap tobacco labor, many of these servants, contracted for four- to six-year terms, were escaping the crowded, impoverished conditions of seventeenth-century England. The bulk of the Chesapeake's indentured servants fit the description of the boy buried in the cellar: young lower- to middle-class men, spurred by Britain's harvest failures and explosive population growth, who left behind a country where as much as half the population lived below the poverty line.[22] In return for the cost of their Atlantic passage, food, board and lodging, they worked as contracted laborers, usually living closely with the family or individual who held their contract.

It was a hard, sometimes brutal way to forge a new path. Although only a teenager, the boy's remains indicated that he suffered from tuberculosis when he died. There were several herniated disks in his back, injuries incurred from extremely hard physical labor. The Leavy Neck servant's premature decrepitude would have been unsurprising in the Chesapeake frontier. Young, hale men were routinely transformed into ropey workhorses by the meager diet, the hard work and chronic disease. What was also unsurprising was the little respect given to his burial. The region was flooded with seemingly endless tides of ambitious strangers, each of whom had given away multiple years of their autonomy to unknown individuals. Those that succumbed to sickness or toil were easily replaced. Here, life was cheap.

Wedged into a tiny grave, the hasty interment of the indentured servant buried at Leavy Neck was evidence of his worthlessness to his contracted

The Leavy Neck boy as recreated for a 2009 exhibit at the Smithsonian Institution. *Image by Smithsonian Institution.*

family. The body in the cellar showed no indication of formality or respect, with his legs and arms crammed awkwardly into the narrow hole and the layers of rotting oyster shell tossed casually on top of him. The life of this boy, like one described in *Leviathan* by the seventeenth-century British philosopher Thomas Hobbes, was "solitary, poor, nasty, brutish, and short."

By the end of the seventeenth century, as the birth rate in England began to dwindle, the steady influx of indentured workers slowed. This was a serious problem in the Chesapeake, where land was abundant but the hands needed to cultivate it were terribly scarce. Tobacco, the lucrative but tedious harvest, remained the lifeblood of the region, representing the single economy and source of all trade: "Tobacco is our meat, drinke, cloathing, and monies," wrote Hugh Jones in 1699. The manpower needed to grow the crop would need to be found elsewhere—and for the first time, slaves became the single obvious answer for the Chesapeake's perpetual labor problem.[23]

African slaves were not new to the Chesapeake. The first documented arrival of slaves was in 1619 at Jamestown, hardly ten years after the initial settlement. During the height of the indentured servant system, most of these slaves were Creoles from the Caribbean region, but as the concentration of new arrivals from Britain declined, the slaves that were sold in the Chesapeake were abducted from the southern coast of Africa—Eastern Nigeria and West Central Africa.[24]

The slaves who arrived in the Chesapeake were entering a completely foreign world. Unlike slaves of Creole origin, who at least had some familiarity with the large-scale plantations of white owners, Chesapeake slaves in the late seventeenth century would have found themselves in an alien environment ruled by tobacco. In the one hundred years since the outpost at Jamestown was created, the deep, clear tributaries of the southern Bay had become briskly traversed arteries, carrying tobacco and people locally and internationally. Huge tracts of land adjacent to the water were dedicated to tobacco cultivation that, unlike most of European farming, was focused around the hoe rather than the plow. Tobacco, known as the "sixteen month crop," required an incredible effort to send to market, with each plant individually tended and coaxed to full leaf. Plantation owners frequently worked the fields themselves, but to expand their fields and profits, they needed ever more manpower to meet Europe's ceaseless clamor for the sotweed.

On the Chesapeake's plantations, slaves were a grim if banal solution to the constant need for labor. Most seventeenth-century planters could afford only one or perhaps two slaves, which, in the interest of economizing, lived closely with their owners in dismal little earthen-floored dwellings.[25] Though intimately connected in close quarters and through the everyday routines of work, eating and sleeping, there were deep distinctions between slaves and their masters—differences that intensified as the period of indentured servitude ended. While the seventeenth century had afforded slaves some of the same privileges enjoyed by indentured servants, by the beginning of the eighteenth century, those sharply waned. Besides rest days, slave owners were under no obligation to provide other niceties that English servants had seen as basic rights: enough food of decent quality, adequate clothing and shelter.[26]

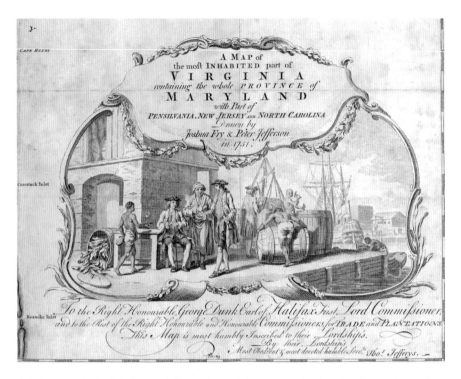

A 1751 map of Virginia featured illustrations of slaves preparing hogsheads of tobacco for trade. *Library of Congress Collections.*

The proximity of Chesapeake tobacco plantations to waterways did provide a few benefits to the slaves who toiled on meager rations—the rivers represented an alternate source of easily accessed food. Coastal dwellers, the Chesapeake's newly arrived slaves found that some aspects of the landscape were recognizable, if not familiar. The western coast of Africa is interlaced with extensive brackish river systems like those branching off the Bay's main stem, where the waterways provided transportation routes and abundant opportunities for harvesting seafood and shellfish. Mangrove oysters, *Crassostrea gasgar*, were an important element of the traditional diet in these African coastal communities, where dugout canoes not unlike those made by the Chesapeake's native communities plied the rivers.[27] Free, familiar and unlimited, oysters and other seafood made up a significant proportion of the Chesapeake slave diet from the seventeenth century onward. Even as their masters ultimately moved away from foraging wild species in favor of a menu boasting domesticated animals and vegetables grown in kitchen gardens, slaves remained masters of making do, foraging in the fields and forest of their surrounding environment.

Oysters also offered opportunities for pinpricks of freedom in an otherwise bleak life of toil. Harvesting oysters for their owners frequently became slaves' work. Oysters were accessed by foot along shorelines at low tide or in small vessels, like the region's dugout canoes, which slaves paddled or poled to nearby shoals. A French visitor to Virginia, Durand de Dauphine, observed in 1686 that to get as many oysters as he wanted, he "only had to send one of [the] servants in one of the small boats & two hours after ebb-tide he brought back full. These boats made of a single tree hollowed in the middle, can hold as many as fourteen people & twenty-five hundredweight of merchandise."[28]

Even the spent shell from consumed oysters found value for Chesapeake slaves. As slaves began to create families and plantations grew during the early eighteenth century, field workers were moved out of the dwellings of their masters into concentrated quarters. There they had a bit of control over their living spaces and began to infuse them with traditional elements, like swept-earth yards and oyster shell paths. Although oyster shells made popular filler for the invariably muddy paths of all classes, slaves valued them for their distinctive crunch underfoot.[29] Anyone treading on oyster shells would noisily make themselves known, giving slaves advance warning of someone approaching, whether friend or master.

According to Jane Cox, most planters along the waterfront owned their own small watercraft by this period—a boon for slaves who found autonomy on the water unknown on the land. "Knowing what's in the archaeological record, like fish bones and copious amounts of oyster shell everywhere, boats were integral to what people needed to survive. Everybody's got their own access to the water in this period, and each generation would pass down their shotgun and their boat to your son because those were like heirlooms for survival." Slaves navigating these vessels to gather up a few days' worth of oysters could easily put some aside that might be sold or traded to neighbors or dockside in the few larger communities like Williamsburg, St. Mary's City and, later, Annapolis.

In this quiet way, the Chesapeake's slaves became the first commercial watermen. The money or goods they received as payment from their oysters were one of their only means of making income independently of their owners, whether it was saved or spent on small luxuries. Their foraging and fishing also created a deep, intimate knowledge of the landscape and layout of the tributaries among the enslaved population. This encompassing understanding of the region and easy access to watercraft was an asset for slaves, especially ones who wanted to escape. "Committed to the gaol at Westmoreland," read an advertisement for runaways from 1771, "...two Negro men, one a yellow fellow with a remarkable split nose, the other black, with filed teeth. Both are Africans and speak very little English. They are supposed to have run from Maryland, as there was a large canoe found near the place they were taken."

As the seventeenth century turned into the eighteenth century, the Chesapeake's population continued to grow, buoyed by the first and second generations of Chesapeake-born children of immigrants, both free and enslaved. By 1700, there were ninety-four thousand colonists living in Maryland and Virginia, and of that number, one-sixth were slaves.[30] The small clusters of homes and people once dismissed by Lord Baltimore as "barely Townes" were beginning to grow into communities of substance, with large, permanent populations. Water-oriented sites, places like Williamsburg and St. Mary's City, remained deeply reliant on the Bay's resources.

Modern archaeologists have even been able to track the rise—and in St. Mary's City, after the capital was moved to Annapolis, the fall—of these towns through the oyster shells they discarded along the way. Founded in 1634, St. Mary's City reached its largest size in the 1680s and 1690s, when it had its peak population at around two hundred permanent residents and many more seasonally when the Assembly met. The shape of the nearby oyster shoals that fed the community would have changed significantly over time as more oysters were harvested in the boom years to meet the demand. The oldest oysters at the site found today are large—the average size from hinge to bill is around eighty millimeters, about the size of an adult human's palm—indicating the St. Mary's City dwellers were harvesting from an oyster reef slowly enough that oysters could grow to a heftier size. By the peak of the city's population, that shell size had fallen to only thirty millimeters on average, indicating that the demand increased so much that small oysters were being gathered before reaching a more substantial length. After the capital was moved to Annapolis in 1695, the population dropped, and oyster shells returned to a generous eighty millimeters again.[31]

Oyster shell size around this period also indicates the arrival of a new tool to harvest oysters. Up until this point, oysters could be largely gathered by hand or with small rakes. The oyster reefs, layered over thousands of years, created hard shoals that colonists might walk on with stout boots to take as many oysters as they needed. But over years of heavy harvest, those topmost, easily reached oysters were taken, and the height of the oyster shoals began to dwindle. Oyster tongs, two oyster rakes connected by their handles to make a scissor-like tool, helped to reach down into water too deep for standing, where lower layers of the oyster reef thrived. A Swiss visitor to Virginia in 1702, Francis Louis Michel, wrote home about his observations of the topography, people and environment. In particular, he meticulously documented the oysters reefs and the tongs used to work them:

> *The abundance of oysters is incredible. There are whole banks of them so that the ships must avoid them. A sloop, which was to land us at Kingscreek, struck an oyster bed, where we had to wait about two hours for the tide. They surpass those in England by far in size, indeed, they are four times as large. I often cut them in two, before I could put them into my mouth.*
>
> *The inhabitants usually catch them on Saturday. It is not troublesome. A pair of wooden tongs is needed. Below they are wide, tipped with iron. At the time of the ebb they row to the beds and with the long tongs they reach down to the bottom. They pinch them together tightly and then pull or tear up that which has been seized. They usually pull from six to ten times. In summer they are not very good, but unhealthy and cause fever.*[32]

Eighteenth-century oysters, as indicated by Michel's account, indicate that even in this era, the oyster's seasonality was respected. Oysters spawn in the summer, and their thin, milky consistency during the warm months was much less preferable than in the wintertime, when their fat flesh reached its most toothsome. Those who trespassed on these rules drew comment, such as Landon Carter in 1776, who requested a large quantity of oysters in July, "But I was asked why Beale sent up oysters in July. I answered it was my orders. Who would eat oysters in July said the mighty man?"[33]

Out-of-season shellfish were not only unpalatable. Especially in the summer, rivers, which were used by Bay towns as self-flushing sewers, could proliferate with bacteria. Summer oysters carried the possibility of then-unidentified diseases like typhoid or dysentery. Colonial communities had no name for the water-borne diseases, considered "bilious" illnesses, that killed with a deadly potency. That tradition has carried forward to the modern era in the form of the "R"-month rule that many in the region still observe. Unaware of the origins of this ingrained ritual, communities around the Chesapeake continue to only eat oysters in the cold months of the year from September to April, even though modern sanitation practices have made it safer to consume oysters year-round.

# CHESAPEAKE OYSTERS

The high consumption of oysters was vital to the success of the Chesapeake colony not only because of the bellies they filled. Oysters in many cases literally formed the foundation of many of the better sort of the Bay's brick architecture. As cities formed, and plantations grew in prosperity over several generations, the wooden shanties hastily erected in the colony's early years were replaced with rosy brick edifices meant to convey wealth and status. Lacking limestone, burned oyster shells provided the quicklime needed in both mortar and plaster, and oyster-based quicklime became the cement that held colonial cities together.

The market for oyster shells grew along with the building boom in new cities like Williamsburg and Annapolis. Oyster shells were also an essential component of iron making, another critical element for the expanding cities of the Chesapeake colony, and advertisements requesting new sources of shells appear frequently in eighteenth-century newspapers. In the *Virginia Gazette* on February 11, 1768, John Holladay, whose ironworks sold pig, bar and cast iron, sought "a large quantity of OYSTER SHELLS…for which ready money, dry goods, or iron may be had." One advertisement from the *Federal Gazette* on March 3, 1790, offers both oyster shells and slaves skilled at iron making for sale: "At a private sale, upwards of 30 negroes, consisting of men, women and children, amongst whom are several very valuable colliers and laborers, also a quantity of oyster shells and charcoal."

As the towns of the Chesapeake colonial world expanded in the eighteenth century, so did the diets of most people living along the waterways. No longer just a subsistence culture focused only on survival, the tables of tidewater colonists now regularly included imported items that were once considered luxuries, like sugar and tea, as well as the hallmarks of civilization as the English knew them—beef and pork. In general, consumption of fish declined significantly as animals "on the hoof" were consumed instead—in post-1700 archaeological sites, domesticated species make up 90 percent of the animal bones in the trash middens.[34] The fish that do show up in the table scraps of the region are increasingly the kind harvested in nets, like herring or bluefish. Oysters, however, remained entrenched, both in the trash piles and Chesapeake's colonial foodways.

Archaeologists' shovels and trowels aren't the only useful tools for understanding exactly how much Chesapeake colonists liked oysters. Cookbooks became much more commonly available in Bay communities during the 1700s, and these imported British recipes greatly influenced the tables and kitchens of eighteenth-century Virginia and Maryland. England was still in many regards the gold standard of culture and civilization, and "receipts" in eighteenth-century cookbooks show the continuing popularity of oysters across the ocean and therefore locally, as well. Oysters' delicate flavor made them a versatile ingredient, and English cookbooks provided endless ways to prepare them, from simple pies, fritters and stews to elaborate dishes with veal, egg or even, in one notable example, oyster ice cream.

By far the most popular source of oyster recipes of the eighteenth-century Chesapeake was Hannah Glasse's *Art of Cookery Made Plain and Easy*. Written simply in accessible language, it was first published in 1727 in London and in 1742 in Williamsburg—it was the first cookbook published in the American colonies—and was used continuously afterward for a century. While many of the recipes include flavor pairings unfamiliar to a modern palate—nutmeg and mace, for example, are regularly used to flavor savory dishes—Glasse's suggestions for oyster recipes mostly include ingredients and food preparation that continue to be used today. One main difference, however, are the quantities of shellfish Glasse's recipes call for. When published, these recipes would have been costly in England, where the dense population had taken its toll on the overfished shellfish stocks. In the oyster-rich Chesapeake, however, shellfish were cheap staples suitable for the working classes, and these popular recipes would have been affordable for even modest tables.

In her recipe for "A Ragoo of Oysters," Glasse offers a thickened stew, flavored with beef stock and white wine and studded with fried oysters—a dish tasty enough to regularly grace the stylish table of the governor of Virginia. Chef Frank Clark knows this recipe well—there's even a video on Youtube of Clark, in eighteenth-century garb, capably preparing the dish. Clearly, Clark is no ordinary chef. As the head of Colonial Williamsburg's respected Historic Foodways department, he oversees a staff of five interpreters who research and replicate eighteenth-century Chesapeake recipes for a living.

Each day, they prepare various dishes in authentic colonial fashion, laboriously translating inscrutable period receipts into meals that George Washington would recognize. While some of the other spaces at Colonial Williamsburg have the sense of a two-dimensional stage set, the department's base of operations—the kitchens at the Governor's Palace—lean sharply toward the "living" side of "living history." Crackling with messy activity and radiant heat, and laced with the smells of roasting meat and woodsmoke, Clark's kitchens are anything but museum pieces.

"We've got lots of great oyster recipes in eighteenth-century cookbooks," Clark says, entering his second-story office above the kitchens below. Here, some anachronisms are permitted to infringe on the eighteenth-century

Williamsburg Historic Foodways director Frank Clark. *Image by author.*

illusion on the first floor—well-thumbed modern cookbooks splayed over desks, their bindings splattered with grease; binders of reference materials; supply order forms; dirty aprons. Clark, ignoring the clutter, turns to the bookshelf to hunt for his favorite oyster resources. Over his shoulder, he continues: "And they're buying them pretty frequently here at the Palace. They remain pretty much affordable throughout the eighteenth century. At one point, you could buy eight bushels of oysters for the cost of a dozen oranges."

Not all of these oysters were fresh, however. One of the popular ways to preserve oysters in the eighteenth century was through pickling—cooked oysters bobbing in a mixture of vinegar, wine, salt and spices. So popular was pickling, in fact, that large quantities of pickled oysters were prepared and shipped to ports both local and distant. "Barrels of pickled oysters were very common," Clark confirms. "There are lots of descriptions in the cookbooks of how to do it, and so on. I believe there were some stored on this property, as well, when the governor died and they did the inventory." Period accounts echo Clark's research. Landon Carter in 1776 recorded in his diary, "Last night my cart…brought me eight bushels oysters. Out of the eight bushels I had six pickled and two bushels for dressing."[35]

Pickled oysters apparently also made a gift rarefied enough for a president. In a letter from Mount Vernon in 1786, George Washington wrote to his friend George Taylor, "Mrs. Washington joins me in thanking you for your kind present of pickled oysters which were very fine. The mark of your politeness is flattering and we beg you to accept every good wish of ours in return."[36]

Hannah Glasse provides a recipe for this colonial staple in her *Art of Cookery Made Plain and Easy*, and the sheer volume of the main ingredient is testament to the popularity of this method of preservation. "To pickle Oysters, Cockles, and Muscles, take two hundred oysters, the newest and best you can get; then put all the liquor and oysters into a kettle, boil them about hour an hour, skimming them as the scum rises." Once cooked, Glasse recommends the oyster be strained and spiced with mace and cloves before finally stored in a barrel, covered with salt, white-wine vinegar and pepper.

Oysters prepared this way might keep up to a month, unrefrigerated. Admittedly, the combination of warm, free-floating oysters, vinegar and spices more commonly used in modern sweets sounds unappealing to modern tastes. But Frank Clark says that's typical of the era. In general, our eighteenth-century predecessors had developed tastes borne of limited food preservation techniques, and the vinegar, sugar and spices used to mask turned food eventually became favored flavorings. Pickled oysters were no exception. "They're just eating them straight, rather than really cooking with them much. It sounds terrible, but colonists were willing to eat a lot of things that we find rather disgusting these days."

Eighteenth-century Chesapeake denizens didn't have to eat their oysters alone. In busy taverns across the region, oysters were usually on the menu. Archaeologists excavating these establishments have found dense layers of shell thickly ringing the foundation or filling in disused cellars. Taverns and the food, drink and lodgings they provided played a vital role in public life in the seventeenth- and eighteenth-century Chesapeake. Travel in those centuries was long and arduous, with multi-week journeys taking place over ferry-borne water routes interspersed with muddy roads little better than deer paths. Taverns provided road-weary travelers with a stable for their horses, a bed and a warm meal. The quality of any or all of these amenities could greatly vary from tavern to tavern, however. Visitors had no expectation of a private room, for example, and frequently, even a private, vermin-free bed was too much to ask. Travelers writing letters to their family and friends back home often commented on their lodgings.

Charlotte Browne, traveling through Virginia and Maryland in 1757 with Braddock's army, documented her experiences at local taverns, which supplied luxurious fare, including oysters: "[My brother and self] Went to the Kings Arms and breakfasted…Had for Dinner a Ham & Turkey, a Breast of Veal and Oysters, to drink Madeira Wine, Punch, and Cyder…At 6 we came to the old Court House [now Coleman's ordinary] 17 miles from Bellhaven. Laid in a Room with but 3 beds in it."[37]

Taverns provided shelter and sustenance for travelers and were also gathering places for locals who wanted to enjoy a little liquid refreshment. The potency and quantity of alcohol imbibed by colonists in the seventeenth and eighteenth centuries was extraordinary. In an era before sterilization or public sanitation, water was unsafe to drink, and alcohol in differing strengths was the go-to substitute for adults as well as children. Used to consuming high-test alcohol casually and in large quantity, it is no surprise that the bills run up on accounts at Chesapeake taverns could be staggering. In 1702, one Maryland tavern proprietor took a customer to court for running up an impressive bill during several epic benders. During just one evening in October, the defendant washed down one plate of oysters with a quart of beer followed by three more mugs of beer, a quart of "flip"—a potent cocktail made with brandy and egg—and a quarter of a pint of rum.

During her work in Anne Arundel County, Jane Cox has excavated several tavern sites. One of the taverns was located in London Town—now a museum and heritage garden—where it served a settlement of three hundred people on the Severn River for about sixty years. A thriving colonial village before Annapolis was created just a few miles upstream, London Town was one of the most important tobacco ports in Maryland in the late seventeenth and early eighteenth centuries, and its large tavern would haven been well trafficked by locals and travelers alike.

Like the court records of period tavern bills, the archaeological digs at London Town's tavern site indicated a lot of drinking. Impressive amounts of broken glassware were found in the tavern's old cellar, which had become a convenient dump location after a new cellar was constructed. Along with remains from pricey meals of beef, pork and mutton, the guests' trash showed that oysters were popular. Cox found so many oyster shells in the tavern's cellar that the compressed deposit created a kind of oyster time capsule. Cox remembered the excavation as an experience verging on time travel: "We were peeling the shell back, and it literally smelled like a rotting oyster pile from last weekend. It lasted maybe a minute or two before it finally dissipated. It was a fleeting moment, and you had to be right in the pit with the oysters, but for a little bit, you could smell 1720."

As Annapolis and Baltimore swelled in the mid-eighteenth century, there was plenty of local and regional competition for London Town's tavern. A rather obsequious George Willis, publican, placed a Baltimore advertisement in 1784 to announce

> OYSTER SUPPERS, at the Rising Sun, Next door to the Play-House. The subscriber, who by the inclemency of the weather, has been deprived of the Satisfaction of obliging Customers with Oyster Suppers…the Public may depend upon being furnished with such Suppers with the greatest Despatch, and agreeable Taste, during the Season—hoping that the Excellence both of his Oysters and Liquors, added to his constant Exertions to please, will gain him further encouragement.

Oysters—pickled, fresh, eaten on the half shell or discarded underfoot, ragoo'ed, loaved and fried—were woven into the warp and weft of colonial Chesapeake life. As small Bay outposts transformed into waterfront cities, the role of oysters in the most basic elements of life—food, shelter, work, community—remained constant. What did not, however, was the Chesapeake itself.

As many of the Bay's tobacco farms began to move away from the stagnating tobacco markets to the new cash crop, wheat, plows plunged into the arable lands of the watershed for the first time. This new agricultural practice began what would become one of the Chesapeake's largest environmental issues to the present day—erosion and siltation. The plowed wheat fields with their exposed furrows of soil allowed topsoil to wash away with every rain. As the growing shipbuilding industry began to eat into the once-dense forests of oak and pine, erosion accelerated.

# CHESAPEAKE OYSTERS

By the time of the Revolutionary War, there were between fifteen to twenty foundries and almost thirty operational shipyards in Maryland alone, all deforesting their surrounding landscapes at a tremendous rate.[38] The rivers began to choke on the free-flowing soil that sluiced off the land. Harbors that were once deep enough to accommodate the hulls of oceangoing ships began to get shallower and shallower as their bottoms filled with silt. In a span of fifty years, formerly deep-water ports like Bladensburg, Port Tobacco and Joppa transformed from maritime hubs to virtually landlocked communities as the rivers choked with mud.

Oysters, as filter feeders, can be natural remedies of a sort for suspended sediment. Constantly feeding, they draw water through their bodies and digest algae, dispose of dirt or particles in neat balls and release a clarified stream of water back into the environment. One oyster can scrub up to fifty gallons of water a day, and the millions that thrived in the Chesapeake in the eighteenth century would have been able, at least temporarily, to help balance the Bay's environmental equilibrium. But the explosion of population growth, the continuing hunger for land and the popularity of the Chesapeake oyster would only continue to grow as the eighteenth century moved inexorably into the nineteenth. In Chesapeake rivers, the thick oyster shoals began to quietly drown under clouds of settling topsoil.

# Chapter 4

# WHITE GOLD

In the early eighteenth century, Baltimore gave little indication that it was destined to become a teeming oyster capital, full of immigrants and smokestacks, railroads and factories. A sketch of Baltimore in 1752 showed a cluster of dwellings and fields in a rolling landscape. Focused around a shallow-water harbor, tobacco grew in a fenced plot and men pulling a seine net waded ashore. Bucolic and pastoral, nothing about the scene belies its near future as a waterfront boomtown. The first census of the town, taken that same year, listed thirty names.

In only thirty years, the town did grow substantially—part of a national trend that saw the colonies on the Eastern seaboard expanding nearly ten times between 1700 and 1775.[39] By 1774, "Baltimore Town" boasted 564 houses and 5,934 inhabitants in a community where three separate villages—Baltimore Town, Fell's Point and Jones Town—had eventually been knitted together by rapid growth.[40] It was a dramatic transformation. The waterfront remained, as in the 1752 sketch, the central focus around which the city expanded—the beating heart of the Chesapeake flush with trade, food and resources. The city's surrounding marshes were filled in as the hungry demand for wharf space persisted.

As the century turned from the eighteenth to the nineteenth, the same critical elements of life in Baltimore were unchanged—the waterfront was the focus from which the city's diverse population and structure radiated.

Huge wharfs and dock structures extended into the harbor, bristling with the masts of local, regional and international sailing vessels. No longer under British rule, the nineteenth-century Americans in Baltimore flourished, expanding into the growing markets of cotton and powder milling. The city's rapid growth represented vitality and progress but did not necessarily mean sophistication. A visiting Frenchman in the late 1790s, Ferdinand-Marie Bayard, sniffed, "Few of the streets are paved; the great quantity of mud after a rain, everything announces that the air must be unhealthful. However, if you ask the inhabitants they will tell you no." Of the vital wharves from which the city drew its economic might, Bayard commented, "They are constructed from the trunks of trees. When the tide falls it exposes a slime which gives off foul vapors…There are no public or private buildings which are better than second rate."

Baltimore had no pretentions. It wasn't a European city; it was a Chesapeake one—rawboned, with a skeleton of muddy streets and brackish blood. Unrefined but brash and successful, Baltimore was a city built on infusions of new immigrants and industry, awash in the Bay's bounty. Oystering would become one of those industries, with the power to make fortunes and take lives, all part of a day's work. But it would take a massive transition of demand and production for the sleepy mainstay economy of shellfish to truly take off.

Baltimore in the early nineteenth century, though significantly expanded, still straggled behind Philadelphia, New York or Boston. Baltimore's population was much smaller, and though the city boasted a flourishing shipbuilding industry oriented around the Fell's Point neighborhood, it was still only an upstart in terms of commerce. Its oystering business was no exception. Baltimore's Fish Market, adjacent to the larger Marsh Market, was bustling with vendors proffering all sorts of things harvested from the Chesapeake, including oysters. Serviced by oystermen white and black, free and enslaved, who took small craft out to oyster shoals and harvested with tongs, it was the largest trade in shellfish the Bay had ever seen. It still wasn't much, however, when compared to New York's massive Fly Market or the endless rows of stalls at Boston's Dock Square.

The fate of the Chesapeake's early oyster economy was inextricably linked to its connections with New England. Still deeply local at the beginning of the nineteenth century, northern rumblings were about to change what remained a modest oyster harvest. Unlike the Chesapeake, whose expansive tributaries had encouraged a widely distributed population throughout the seventeenth and eighteenth centuries, the forbidding coastline of New

England favored towns with proximity to the sea. Although the Chesapeake had been settled first, it was New England that established the first major colonial metropolises, founded on the endlessly flowing silver river of cod, herring, mackerel and alewives.

Residents in New England communities had the same penchant for shellfish as their Chesapeake counterparts, and oysters represented a familiar and easy source of protein. Their abundance also mirrored the enormous oyster reefs first observed by Virginia's settlers. Yet the demand for oysters in New England's flourishing cities was so bottomless that quickly, the oyster reefs were stripped. As early as 1679, a city ordinance in Brook Haven, New York, restricted the number of vessels allowed to harvest oysters.[41] Similar regulations followed in many other coastal communities, limiting tools, outlawing the removal of shell "cultch," restricting the harvest to locals only, enforcing size requirements or closing summer harvests to encourage spawning.

The enormous consumption of oysters in New England was facilitated by new technology. "Draggs" or what would later be called "dredges" in the Chesapeake were employed in New England during the eighteenth century—essentially, a triangular iron frame with rake-like teeth along one edge and a rope net across the back. These heavy tools were lowered overboard and towed behind sailing vessels where they would scrape over oyster beds, gathering up large quantities of oysters. The upside of dredges was their efficiency—one sailing vessel with a dredge could do the work of five tongers in a day. That sizeable catch could then be loaded onto small sailboats known as "smacks" and sent to the ravenous oyster markets in New York City.[42]

The downside of dredges was that same efficiency—a sailing fleet harvesting oysters with dredges could quickly strip a productive bed of all its mature oysters in a season or two. But the potential for profits was far more seductive than the calls for oystering restraint—dredges, and the enterprising captains who employed them, took a swift and dramatic toll on New England's oysters. As early as 1766, Rhode Island outlawed the use of dredges, and several other New England colonies quickly followed suit.

It proved fruitless. As early as the beginning of the nineteenth century, the oyster beds in New England were all but barren. This put New England in the unprecedented American position of having to decide: once you have overharvested a species, what do you do next? The first solution proposed was to just source oysters from other places where they were abundant. The Chesapeake Bay was the obvious location. And so began what was known in New England as the "Virginia trade," where the Bay's oysters were harvested, loaded on schooners and delivered to ports like New Haven for direct sale. Later this model was revised to include a seasonal Virginia oyster stop-off on a sandbar over the summer months to allow for extra "fattening."[43] The first documented trip bound from New Haven for the Virginia oyster trade was officially 1830, although activity occurred as early as 1808 from southern ports in New Jersey.[44]

The fact that New England's port cities viewed the Chesapeake Bay as their own oyster bank account was not lost on the Virginians, who then, as now, strongly disliked meddlesome outside ventures. The dredge in particular was regarded with distrust. Fed up with New England profiting from Virginia's oyster beds, Virginia moved to outlaw the newfangled technology in 1811. Undeterred, the captains from New Haven simply turned their vessels north toward the Maryland side of the Chesapeake. Maryland reacted in a similar fashion as their neighbors with regard to the northern interlopers. In 1820, the state enacted its first oyster law, making dredges illegal and requiring that oysters only be transported out of state in ships owned by Maryland residents for at least a year.

The New Englanders were nothing if not calculating. As Chesapeake residents attempted to use regulations as a way to wall off their oyster bounty, the New Haven captains were of the mind that when opportunity closed a door, it opened a window. If regulations required state residency to transport oysters out of Maryland waters, then the solution was simple—move to Maryland.

Caleb Maltby was one of these enterprising New Haven oyster businessmen to set down roots in Baltimore. Unlike his New England transplant counterparts, he sought a more economical way to harness the untapped oyster riches of the Chesapeake. Shipping Maryland or Virginia oysters to back to New Haven for processing was unnecessarily time consuming and expensive. Why not simply harvest, pack and ship oysters directly from Baltimore instead? Acting on this line of typically pragmatic Yankee thinking, Maltby established what would be the first oyster packinghouse in the Chesapeake between 1834 and 1835.[45]

Oysters were not the only Baltimore resource that Maltby cleverly utilized. In England, a revolutionary new technology had been developed in 1804—the steam locomotive. Designed to replace the teams of packhorses that had been used to laboriously shuttle coal from mines to ports, the newfangled locomotive achieved breakneck speeds of nine miles per hour. It was an idea of staggering import, eclipsing water travel as the swiftest means of transporting good or people. America, which had been largely focused on building canals as a means of extending its transportation network, saw the opportunity. In reaction to a newly proposed canal system connecting Washington, D.C., to the Ohio River (the C&O Canal) that would bypass Baltimore, a group of savvy Baltimore businessmen proposed to charter a competing railroad on February 28, 1827. It would become the legendary Baltimore and Ohio railroad—the first commercial rail line in the United States.

By Maltby's day, the B&O railroad—which had belatedly introduced a steam locomotive to accompany the rail line in 1831—was operational and growing, with lines extending to Washington, D.C. Initially, Maltby—not just fiscally conservative—declined to use the service. Instead, he established a

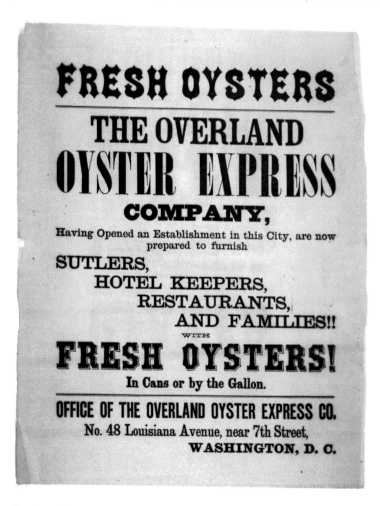

Overland Oyster Express advertisement for rail line to Washington, D.C. *Library of Congress Collections.*

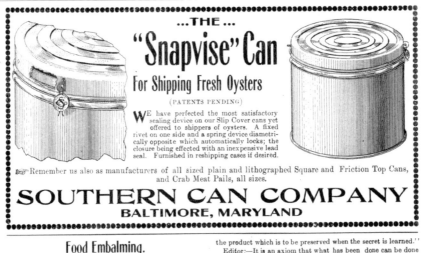

## Food Embalming.

Portland, Ore.—William H. Swet, of this city, claims to have rediscovered the lost Egyptian art of preserving vegetable and animal matter indefinitely.

He has taken roses and let them wither since last summer. Then the petals, moistened, resumed the original freshness and color and the withered buds burst into blossom. Corn on the cob, which had dried into a third its former size, was restored merely by being placed in water over night, so that it not only looked but tasted fresh, Other vegetables were similarly demonstrated.

Swett says that in so far as comparison is possible he has succeeded in securing suspended disintegration in the products he prepares. He operates a queer looking apparatus. A fire burns in both ends of an oblong case. Horizontal screen slides bear the preserving product. Air constantly circulates within.

"I have been experimenting for fifteen years seeking for the element which successfully applied, kept disintegration from affecting food products." he said Several years ago, by chance, I happened upon the effects. So sometimes the things I turned out would keep indefinitely, sometimes they soured. I did not know the cause. It is that cause which I have now discovered. It is an element that permeates the air. A child may apply it to the product which is to be preserved when the secret is learned."

Editor;—It is an axiom that what has been done can be done again. Thus the discovery of Mr. Swet, not being a new thing, is demonstrable. What a boon to the grower to have his product kept fresh indefinitely. Let us see now how this works out. We learn that a certain New Jersey man has a solution in which he immerses the oyster in the shell, and it will keep for a month in transit. Now all these discoveries seem to have come to help the unfortunate oystermen out of his Pure Food trouble. Let these men come forward now and convince our illustrious Dr. Wiley and then we will all be happy.

A Vancouver, B. C., dispatch says: The provincial government, through Deputy Commissioner of Fisheries Babcock, has notified certain salmon canners in Vancouver that it is now considering the question of withholding operating licenses until such time as the canners reach an agreement as to limiting the number of boats fished by canneries. The operating licenses are those known as cannery licenses and the right of the province to license for revenue purpose is upheld by a decision of the privy council.

The oyster steamer Laura R was launched from Radel's shipyards, Port Jefferso, L. I.

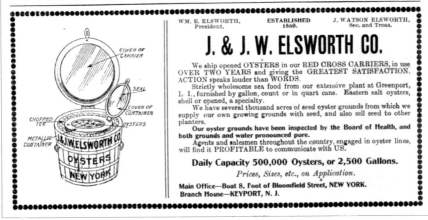

J.W. Elsworth oyster carrier advertisement illustrating a typical method of shipping canned oysters. *Chesapeake Bay Maritime Museum collections.*

line of wagons from Baltimore to Pittsburgh to bring live or pickled oysters past the Appalachian Mountains.[46] That changed, however, as Maltby and his many followers wholeheartedly embraced another European innovation in Baltimore: canning. A technology with the ability to take their oysters nationwide, canning revolutionized food preservation and would ultimately transform Baltimore's harbor from working wharves to industrial mecca.

Nicolas Appert, a Frenchman, invented canning in 1809 after years of research. The French government had offered a prize of 12,000 francs for anyone who could develop a new way for the national army and navy to preserve food, and Appert's invention won. Until then, drying, salting, smoking or pickling were still the only ways to keep food from spoiling. In the case of oysters, pickling was the method that worked for any length of time, but its strong taste appealed to a rather limited audience. The salt and vinegar used in pickling also limited the ways the oysters could be prepared. As in Caleb Maltby's example, the best way to ship oysters in this period was in the shell. Under the right conditions, they might last a week or even two before spoiling, and raw oysters were gustatory chameleons, able to be transformed into endless iterations of fritters, stews or pies. Canning brought all the benefits of oysters in the half shell, with the added bonus of substantially increased shelf life.

The French technology was new to Baltimore in the 1830s but not to the United States. It had first been established in America in New York City in 1812, where wrought-iron cans plated in tin were successfully used to preserve fruits, vegetables and oysters in Robert Ayars's factory. One of Ayars's New York canning contemporaries, a British man named Thomas Kensett, moved to Baltimore and set up his own oyster processing plant on Cove Street in 1849. Again, New England introduced a transformative new technology to the Chesapeake's oyster industry. Kensett was successful and expanded his business to include summer crops, like peaches and tomatoes, that grew on Maryland's arable Eastern Shore. Shrewdly observing Kensett's success, entrepreneurs by the dozen began to open up their own canneries, processing and preserving tons of the Chesapeake's bounty. [47]

Canneries like Kensett's and others required a staggering amount of manpower. The process involved many steps: after unloading oysters from the dockside vessels, they were transported via wheelbarrows or carts into the shucking room. After a light steaming to open the oysters, they were ferried to endless rows of shuckers—usually women—who stood in three-sided, narrow stalls at long tables, deftly plowing through mountains of shellfish. Unlike the smooth finesse of modern-day raw bar shuckers, packinghouse shuckers often used rudimentary techniques to get into the oysters. Armed with flattened pieces of iron for knives, shuckers would knock the bills off to quickly access the adductor muscles holding the shells closed. The shucked meats fell into buckets, and the shells were discarded on either side of the stall, forming drifts several feet high. Full buckets of oysters were whisked away for rinsing and then packed into cans, which fit neatly into buckets with room on top for ice.

At each step along the way, human hands shoveled, shucked, washed and packed the oysters processed in canneries. Long before the concept of a mechanized process or an assembly line, the packinghouses capitalized on Baltimore's incredible abundance of cheap, seemingly endless immigrant labor. German and Irish immigrants poured into the city, seeking refuge from conflicts or famine in their home countries. Packinghouse work was piecework, and while it required skills of a sort, it was the sort of low-wage, high-drudgery employment relegated for the lowest classes. Packinghouses—a cold, wet environment due to the winter oyster season and the oyster themselves—were dismal places to work. This did not prevent children from being pressed into service, however.

Baltimore oyster packinghouse interior, circa 1914. Photograph by Arthur J. Olmstead. *Maryland Historical Society collections.*

An industrial report described average workers in a Baltimore packinghouse: "The oysters are steamed in iron cages, which run on tramways, and the shuckers stand on either side of the long rows of these cages in the oyster house and shuck the oysters into tin cans. The shuckers work in gangs of about eight persons—men, women and children. In busy seasons they can be seen before daylight, waiting at the door of the packinghouse to commence work."

The report described with bureaucratic precision the common prejudices against immigrants during the late nineteenth century: "The oyster shuckers are a very hard working, good-tempered—not very clean—community; their morals are not very strict, if their conversation is a criterion, and the standard of intelligence is certainly low. Their ages range from 12 years up to old men and women. They receive in most houses five cents per can, in others six cents for 4 pounds. They will average 70 cents per day wages."[48]

Thomas Kensett himself was proud to employ children in what he considered the beneficial environment of his packinghouse. In an address to the Baltimore Oyster Packer's Association in 1869, he stated proudly, "Were it not for the shucking of oysters, many children, from twelve to fifteen years of age, would spend much of their time in the streets and around the wharves and docks, being trained up to immorality and crime, and preparing to fill up our jails and warehouses." Kensett's claims aside, images from the period indicate that canneries were hardly the place to foster upstanding youth. Cavernous and gloomy, the oyster canneries were filled with hulking industrial equipment that vented steam and floors carpeted in grimy oyster shells. Kensett's wildly successful oyster packing business, and the dozens of others that nestled cheek-to-jowl along Baltimore's harbor, were perfect examples of the horrors the Industrial Revolution inflicted on its human cogs.

Between 1830 and 1880, canning became Baltimore's second-largest industry. Issac Solomon—who later went on to establish a packinghouse on what would later be known as a major oyster hub, Solomon's Island—allowed canneries to ramp up production by inventing a rapid sterilization process. Packinghouses that once processed three thousand cans a day could now produce twenty thousand, turning an enormous profit and encouraging new seafood processors to start up businesses.[49] Canning's dramatic expansion mirrored that of the railroads, which added nine thousand miles of new rail line by 1850 and redoubled growth again to move troops and supplies during the Civil War.[50] The development of the American railroad system in the nineteenth century impacted far more than merely canneries, however.

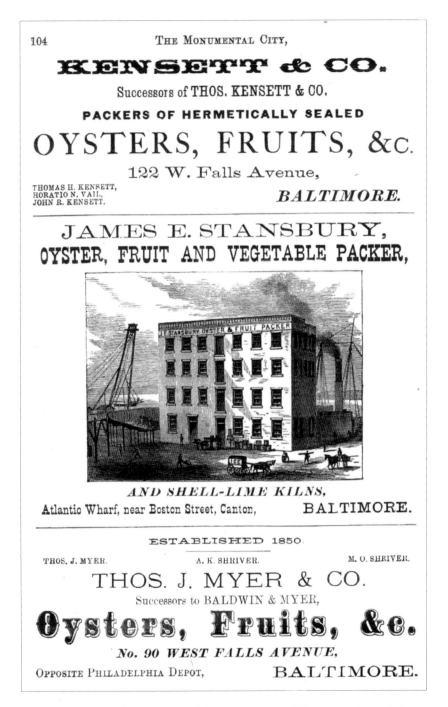

Nineteenth-century advertisement for Thomas Kensett and Company. *Chesapeake Bay Maritime Museum collections.*

It succeeded in doing what arduously constructed roads or even steamboats couldn't—it opened up the West for settlement.

The country's population that once hugged the coastline now began to disperse to interior communities that followed the railroad, advancing past the Mississippi into the plains of the American prairie and beyond. These eastern transplants put down roots in Midwestern towns and cities but they brought many of their traditions and cultural norms with them—including an almost universal penchant for that staple of the maritime diet, oysters. Tiny, one-street towns often boasted an oyster house, while larger cities frequently had many more. Chicagoans, in particular, loved oysters, and nationally regarded oyster palaces like the Boston House—described as "the most perfect and elegant establishment of the kind in the United States" in an 1884 restaurant guide—proliferated in the city.

Supplied by cans—and, as rail transportation became faster, live bushels—of the Chesapeake's sweet, slightly briny shellfish, these establishments boasted oysters in any dish imaginable. Chicago's Boston House offered no fewer than forty-two different oyster preparations to tempt every palate. It was in this era that elaborate recipes were developed, like oysters Rockefeller, which played on the simultaneous popularity of oysters and restaurant dining. Now, instead of laboring over oysters in their home kitchens, patrons might await a decadent meal at their leisure in elegant surroundings. Oysters ragoo, oyster fritters in lemon caper sauce, oysters fricassee, scalloped oysters a la Reine—for diners of the nineteenth century, the oyster was the perfect medium for the era's culinary flights of fancy.

All this oyster consumption, much of it using canned oysters, called for new place settings and silverware. The tastes of the nineteenth century favored complicated tablescapes bristling with specialized forks, knives, spoons and dishes. Often, these were designed to resemble an aspect of the food they were meant to serve—a hallmark of the Victorian fondness for sight gags. Enter the oyster plate. These porcelain dishes, decorated with painted seaweed, jewel-like crabs and painstakingly detailed imitations of oyster shells, were dappled with a half-dozen depressions to serve individual canned oysters.

Oyster plates were meant to rescue shucked oysters from the rather mucosal environment of an oyster can. Evoking a stroll along the seaside, oyster plates elevated their contents to something worthy of crystal decanters and miniature silver forks. Reflecting the ever-expanding availability of Chesapeake oysters thanks to rail, nineteenth-century middle-class hostesses throughout the United States embraced oyster plates as a way to stylishly serve oysters at home.

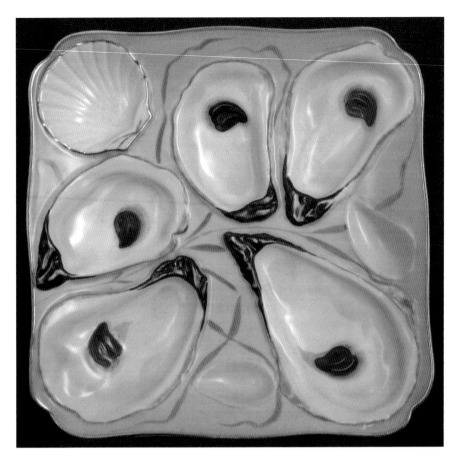

Nineteenth-century oyster plate. *Image by author.*

Porcelain manufacturers produced oyster plates at every price point, and they quickly became a ubiquitous part of the American table. Indeed, when the first Kansas cookbook was printed in 1874, it admonished housekeepers that in order to be properly outfitted, a well-run household should include and oyster service for no fewer than twelve.[51] Today, canned oysters have long since fallen out of fashion. But oyster plates remain, elaborate and disused in dusty little antique shops across the country, a testament to the once-universal place on the table for Chesapeake oysters.

Though the interior of oyster cans were wet, grey masses of oyster meats, the exteriors of oyster cans were sublime. Every rainbow hue was represented, and cans were early marketing works of art that sang the visual praises of the shellfish contained within. From freshness to cleanliness, scenic origins to flavor, each can boasted the uniqueness of its contents as artfully as possible.

The first oyster cans, however, were pure function, zero form. Initially uniformly grey and unadorned, cans were as utilitarian as the wooden buckets they had replaced. As competition grew among oyster canneries, however, savvy businessmen began looking for any way possible to differentiate their brands. One early entrepreneur in the 1860s thought a catchy name might just be the ticket. He dubbed his brand "Cove oysters," which was so memorable it backfired—oyster packinghouses all over Baltimore quickly adopted the name and "cove" oyster quickly became synonymous with *all* canned oysters.[52] With that example in mind, oyster producers learned their lesson—names were not enough. They needed another element—imagery—to really stand out in the sea of shellfish competition.

In the nineteenth century, for the first time in history, pictures were available widely to the public. Just fifty years earlier, most of the American population would have possessed only a few books, and most of those were unillustrated. Newspapers and signage were forests of unrelieved inky text, and the ghostly results of early photography had yet to be invented. Between 1830 and 1880, however, advances were in made in photography and graphic industrial technology that unlocked the visual equivalent of Pandora's box. Images, liberated from the confines of the art gallery, could be reproduced en masse on myriad mediums in rich, saturated color. Combined with the late nineteenth-century development of advertising, another byproduct of the industrial age, by the end of the 1800s, Americans were being bombarded with vibrant graphics on everything from toothpaste boxes to mustard tins.

Oyster cans were no exception. Between 1870 and 1882, developments in lithography turned oyster cans from clunky metallic tubs to into blank canvases. Mermaids, skipjacks, magicians, musicians and storks were all transformed into oyster shills, as one packinghouse after another sought to claim a slice of the market with its brilliantly colored brand. Hand-lettered fonts and persuasive slogans wheedled consumers with their "just a bit better" oysters that "deliciously satisfied" with their "epicure quality." Cooks seeking a quart of oysters would have been overwhelmed by the sheer exuberance of the cans' boisterous colors and claims. It would almost be enough to distract from the fact that the contents were all exactly the same.

The proliferation of canneries was not limited to Baltimore alone. As the railroad reached small Chesapeake towns, whole new areas opened up to the oyster industry. In some cases, sleepy villages like St. Michaels, Maryland, once a hub of the shipbuilding industry in the eighteenth and early nineteenth centuries, were rejuvenated by the arrival of a thriving new economy. Other towns, like Crisfield, Maryland, were created whole cloth by savvy businessmen who speculated on the growth of the oyster industry on an enormous scale. Regardless of location, however, the arrival of the oyster business was a pivotal moment for Chesapeake towns. The Bay's oysters, once practically free, were now white gold—the currency fueling what would later be referred to reverently as the mighty "Chesapeake Oyster Boom."

# CHAPTER 5

# GOD'S OYSTERS

J ohn W. Crisfield was the man responsible for transforming the tiny fishing village of Somer's Cove into Crisfield, the self-proclaimed "Seafood Capital" of Maryland. A wealthy lawyer, congressman and slave owner, Crisfield was a man of power and of means. He was also a man capable of holding two opposing views. As a Southern Unionist during the Civil War, he had worked to keep the South from secession while simultaneously defending slavery, arguing vigorously that slavery's end would spell "degradation, poverty, suffering, and ultimate extinction"[53] for emancipated slaves.

Crisfield was both a staunch defender of the status quo and a savvy speculator in the Chesapeake's future. The Civil War and its repercussions represented enormous upheaval for the Bay's byways. Unlike many of his contemporaries who never recovered as the slave system that had dominated the Chesapeake dissolved, Crisfield sought to harness the change. The railroad, though hugely expanded during the Civil War to transport troops and supplies, still did not reach some of the farthest-flung towns along the Bay's waterways. The Eastern Shore of Maryland and Virginia in particular was deeply isolated, the Chesapeake forming a moat that both protected and prohibited the region from modernizing. Crisfield saw opportunity in what many on the other side of the Bay saw as a backwater and set to the task of bringing the railroad to the Chesapeake's other half.

It was on this lonely peninsula of small towns and tangled rivers that some of the Bay's richest oyster beds lay yet to be touched. In particular, Crisfield set his sights on Somerset County, where the land and the water interlaced in endless marshes and salty shallow islands—possibly the most perfect oyster environment in the Chesapeake Bay. Crisfield's plan was simple—he would bring the railroad to the oysters, and the oysters would make him rich. This idea appealed to other wealthy local investors who also threw their hats into the ring. He proved a shrewd investor, but little did he know that speculation would also gainfully employ thousands of people he would have preferred enslaved. The first train arrived in Somers Cove on November 4, 1866, with the land so low and wet that the end of the tracks stopped awkwardly, well short of an existing steamboat wharf. And so, through the machinations of the well-connected Somerset statesman, Crisfield became the town that oysters built.

The new town boomed. A lighthouse had to be erected in 1867 to manage the new surge of water traffic around the cove's shoals. Packinghouses proliferated along the waterfront, serviced by beamy sailboats that arrived daily, groaning under the weight of hundreds of bushels of oysters. Crisfield's proximity to the prime oystering grounds in the Pocomoke and Tangier

Early twentieth-century Crisfield postcard featuring shipbuilders repairing oyster boats in the harbor. *Chesapeake Bay Maritime Museum Collections.*

sounds assured its future as a hub of the oystering industry, attracting oystermen, shuckers, immigrants, packers and a panoply of businesses to serve the expanding population—many of the sort most frequently seen in frontier towns.

Barber shops, churches and general stores were established on Main Street, which echoed with the sound of hammers on wood as one rambling, gabled house after another was constructed with oyster money. One street over, on Goodsell's Alley, other seedier businesses proliferated on land newly minted from in-filled oyster shells. Saloons, burlesque shows, fighting rings and brothels did busy trade, divesting oystermen from their laboriously earned wages by fist or by flask. Those who profited from the town's morally questionable, get-rich-quick atmosphere handily outnumbered Crisfield's polite society. Often, the two were one and the same. Local saloon keeper Harvey Johnson did double duty as justice of the peace, convening court daily with the announcement: "Gentlemen the court is now in session, but I call attention to the fact that business is still going on at the bar."[54]

In an 1879 *Harper's New Monthly Magazine* article, "The Peninsular Canaan," Crisfield and oysters were synonymous: "A general whiteness illumines the streets of Crisfield; a crisp rattle of loose shells sounds under the tread of the pedestrian; a salt breeze blows in from the beautiful waters of the Tangier Sound, tainted, alas! by a slight odor of defunct oysters. Oysters, oysters everywhere, in barrels, in boxes, in cans, in buckets, in the shell and out." Huge piles of spent oyster shell, sometimes multiple stories high, accumulated over the course of the oystering season in Crisfield and wherever packinghouses operated. Images from the period show magnificent snowdrifts of shell, often dwarfing a tiny human perched on the piles for scale.

Though passerby might have assumed from the rankness of the shell piles that they were garbage, in fact, every bit was used—processed in valuable side businesses that produced oyster shell buttons and bags of ground-shell fertilizer. What wasn't sold or processed became new land. "The town of Crisfield is founded, not upon rock, but upon a bed of oyster shells, thrown into a salt marsh," a *New York Times* article described in 1893. "In this fashion it has slowly marched out into the shallow waters of Tangier Sound, until it seems a shabby little Venice."[55]

Newspapers' rather lyrical descriptions of hardscrabble Crisfield also indicated how dramatically the demographics of the Eastern Shore's packinghouses differed from the large immigrant labor forces of Baltimore. In the *Harper's Weekly* article, accompanying illustrations show African

Piles of oysters at the St. Michaels, Maryland harbor in 1907. Image by Thomas Sewell. *Chesapeake Bay Maritime Museum Collections.*

American women and men bundled up against the frigid temperatures inside the unheated packinghouses and men and boys wheeling barrows of live oysters and spent shell. An 1880 report on the fishery industries of the United States tallied Crisfield's packinghouses at sixteen, and estimated that out of the 678 employees working in those businesses, 500 were black: "Of the packinghouses in Maryland, nearly all of whom are employed in the 'raw' trade, about three-fourths are negroes." The report went on to estimate that in Crisfield alone that year, shuckers had packed 427,270 bushels of oysters.[56]

Unlike Baltimore's early years, when white immigrants had made up the majority of workers at the waterfront packinghouses, by Reconstruction, the Eastern Shore of Maryland and tidewater Virginia had substantial communities of newly emancipated slaves. Many worked year-round in the packinghouses, shucking and shipping oysters in the winter and packing peaches, strawberries and tomatoes in the summer. Working in the packing industry was one of the few options open to Chesapeake African Americans outside of the sharecropping system, but it had plenty

MINE OYSTER—CANNING.

MINE OYSTER—FILLING WITH LIQUOR.

*Harper's Weekly* illustration of Crisfield packinghouse interior, March 1872. *Collections of author.*

of similar drawbacks—including the practice of paying workers "tokens" made of brass, aluminum or, for the truly parsimonious, red fabric instead of paychecks. Some of the larger oyster canneries even had in-house company stores, where these wage tokens could be redeemed for goods—conveniently creating a closed circle of profit for the packinghouse owner and a cycle of dependence for the shucker.

Working on the water ensured a bit more freedom. African Americans, immigrants and white watermen all harvested oysters, many using smaller vessels like the Chesapeake's ubiquitous log canoe to tong their harvest from shoals close to shore. Once the boats were laden with a day's catch, the oysters would then be sold to middlemen on larger buyboats and taken in to the docks in Baltimore, Crisfield, Cambridge or Norfolk, where stevedores would unload the oysters onto carts and take them to the packinghouse.

Unlike packinghouse workers, individual oystermen were generally self-employed, and regardless of an oysterman's race or ethnicity, all got paid the same amount for their catch. Black crews on larger vessels, often owned by packinghouses, had a different experience—they might receive a paltry sum upon being shipped but otherwise could work weeks without pay. Many, for this reason, chose to work singly or in pairs in smaller craft. Water work provided a rather remarkable element of equality and liberty for many African Americans in a region nationally known for its legacy of brutal racism. Although the Chesapeake had once represented a physical escape route for Harriet Tubman, Frederick Douglass and other runaway slaves, it now provided a financial one—in the form of oysters.

Free blacks, immigrants and all able-bodied men not crippled by the great Civil War thronged to the Chesapeake, seeking their fortune in the Bay's still-thick oyster shoals. Gone was the era when oysters were a slow, local harvest—rather, the goal was to limp back into the harbor with water up to the gunwales, decks groaning with oysters piled up to eye level. Tongs were still the traditional technique, but just after the Civil War, Maryland had reconsidered its position on dredges.

Banned since 1820, small, hand-operated oyster dredges known as "scrapes" were legalized in 1854, and full-sized dredges followed in 1865. Along with the dredge legalization came a series of regulations that required dredgers and tongers to purchase oystering licenses, established different regions for tonging and dredging and organized an Oyster Police Force.[57] The legalization of dredges, along with the innovations of canning and the efficient transportation capacities of the post–Civil War era rail, created the perfect storm of demand, capacity and technology for the promising young

African American tongers on the St. Mary's River. *Courtesy of the Mariner's Museum, Newport News, Virginia.*

oyster industry. The ultimate trifecta, together the three combined to ignite the explosive Chesapeake "oyster boom."

Oyster dredges are massive tools and difficult for the modern observer to picture as "innovative technology." Forged from thick iron by blacksmiths, their simple wedge structure and robust teeth look better suited for a castle under siege than the crisp flutes of an oyster's shell. But behind their crude appearance is a tool honed by use and experience, perfectly suited for the brute task of scraping oysters from their beds. Dredges required large vessels with substantial sail power to pull them and a crew of corded, hardy men to wrangle them from bed to deck and back again. In this way, the use of dredges began to change the Chesapeake's traditional oystering culture. Pungies and schooners, long the Bay's signature workhorses, were transformed to suit this new task.

Chesapeake boats were idiosyncratic, often homemade things, full of personalized touches that reflected their uses, their places of origin and the preferences of their owners. These vessels were direct descendants of the

Single-masted log canoes were the oyster vessel of the Chesapeake for more than two hundred years. *Library of Congress Collections.*

indigenous dugout canoes the colonists had adopted, adding sails but not changing much else. The first log canoes were hewn from single, massive trees. Their shallow depth and narrow beam was ideal for the Bay's winding tributaries—much better than the bathtub-like shallops the first settlers awkwardly plowed down southern Chesapeake rivers.

As time went on, large trees were felled for field or firewood. In response, boatbuilders developed a technique of attaching several large logs together, which they then shaped into the slender spear-shape specific to log canoes. These nimble vessels, rakishly proportioned and between twenty and thirty feet long, were perfectly evolved sailing craft for the water-oriented Chesapeake. Easily manned by a crew of one or two, they were all-purpose workhorses used for travel, fishing and hauling. Like our modern pickup trucks, log canoes were one of the essential tools of water work. By 1887, more than 6,300 canoes and skiffs were owned in Maryland and Virginia, employing twelve thousand watermen in oystering.[58]

Chesapeake boats were highly adaptable. In the isolated homesteads throughout the Bay, there were no rules to boatbuilding, no master artisans under whom shipwrights had to apprentice before trying their hand. Experimentation was the rule. In this way, gorgeously evolved boats were built and sailed, growing and expanding to reflect new influences or needs. As the oystering industry waxed in size and profit, so the log canoes did, too—transforming to become the brogan, with two masts and five to seven logs, and, after the legalization of full-sized dredges, the seven- to nine-log bugeye. These massive canoes had enormous sails, which produced enough power to pull the dredges through the oyster beds. They also had centerboards, which could be dropped to prevent drifting on a reach or raised when inevitably the vessel entered a shallow waterway.

For Pete Lesher, the chief curator at the Chesapeake Bay Maritime Museum, the golden era of oystering in the Chesapeake is one of particular fascination. As much as oystering was a product of industrial change, it was also the catalyst for change—particularly in boatbuilding. "My angle into this is the humanistic history of technology and in shipbuilding. We're dealing with an era, like our own, when there's all this innovation going on—boat types, fishing techniques. I find that fascinating—what people are doing to improve their lot in life with this entrepreneurial inventiveness." Chesapeake boats had so few rules that their construction might be tweaked to accommodate changes in the environment or a new way of fishing, often to a very specific end. Lesher explains, "A bugeye does not make a very good yacht. It's not a particularly good freight vessel. It's not good at a whole lot of things, but it's great for oyster dredging. Without understanding this fishery, the whole shipbuilding piece just doesn't make sense."

Lesher has spent his career alternately buried in the yellowing paperwork from this period and its fading copperplate script and in, on and under the splintery remains of the nineteenth- and twentieth-century oystering boats that have survived to the modern day. This two-sided occupation shows in his appearance—scholarly, bespectacled and bow-tie trim, with rolled sleeves that display tanned, strong sailor's arms. This duality has given him unique insight into the evolution of the Bay's oyster boats. He's not only studied them, but he's also sailed them. Despite their often-unbeautiful appearance, Lesher appreciates them as a finely tuned, practical product of their environment.

"When oyster dredging was legalized, you used the boats at hand," Lesher explains, "these pungies—a regional variation on the schooner—as well as Bay schooners and Bay sloops. By 1870, we see this new type appearing on the scene, the bugeye. No one knows where the name comes from, some have suggested the Scottish term for oysters, 'buckie,' but its clear what its describing—an overgrown log canoe, forty-five feet on deck, low to the water. Every aspect of this boat is perfectly adapted for oyster dredging."

Like the nineteenth-century boatbuilders who created the bugeye, Lesher, too, is fond of a vessel that can marry form with function. "I think the bugeye is the prettiest boat out there. It's an elegant little piece. There were pretty bugeyes and there were homely bugeyes out there too—but a well-built bugeye is just about the most attractive boat on the Bay."

If log canoes were pickup trucks, brogans and bugeyes were tractor-trailers—able to haul enormous loads and pull with tremendous power. They were still sail craft, however, and in this era before power engines, they required large crews both in number and in physical size. Oysters—aptly nicknamed "rock" in the Chesapeake—are cumbersome loads with shells that can cut as deeply as a pocketknife. Men working the oysters had to be strapping indeed to raise sails and turn the massive windlass that pulled the dredges, dripping water and cultch, onto the decks of the vessels. Of course, this was wintertime. To follow the oystering rule of thumb, the "R" months are the coldest ones, and bugeyes departing harbors in Solomons,

Baltimore's harbor crowded with large oystering vessels in the late nineteenth century. *Library of Congress Collections.*

Crisfield, Rock Hall and Baltimore would have sailed into leaden skies heavy with snow. If the oysters didn't cut you, the wind certainly would, and the nineteenth-century oilskins and wool were little armor from the freezing spray and constant rewetting of hands and clothing every time the dredges were raised.

The racy lines of a bugeye's proportions that Lesher finds so appealing were not persuasive enough to distract potential crew from the drudgery endured upon the decks. Oystering conditions—icy, wet, terribly dangerous—made it understandably difficult for captains to find a willing crew. Especially in cities, where hundreds of vessels needed thousands of crew every winter, some captains went to extreme measures to find enough able bodies to make it through the season. "Both captains and crews are often the very roughest kind of men. The only ones who do not usually come under this class are the men who live in the oyster districts and hire men from their own localities. On the other hand, fully one-fourth of the men shipped on dredging boats are 'shanghaied,'" reported the *Washington Post* with not a small amount of gleeful voyeurism. "They are made drunk and put on board the boats in stupefied condition. When these men come to their senses they find themselves miles down the river."[59]

Lurid accounts of impressed crew frequently made regional and national headlines in the late nineteenth-century Chesapeake. While these situations were greatly the exception rather than the rule, they happened with enough frequency to catch the eye of journalists and eventually the law. The incentive for captains to rustle up a crew was strong, and ethics were often forgotten when the siren song of profit called. New immigrants were particular targets of shipping agents who took advantage of men fresh off boats from Italy, Germany and Ireland. "The greater number of the men from the shipping agencies are not hard citizens, and most of them not citizens of the United States, but foreigners of the lowest class," reported the *Washington Post*. The article continued, "A shipping agent sees a 'Reuben' walking down the street, approaches him, gains his confidence, and gets him to take a drink. When the man recovers his senses, he finds himself aboard a dredging boat." The outcome could be much worse than just a shanghai and a season's hard labor. "A German on a vessel lying off Swan Point became unruly and the captain attempted to 'enforce the law.' The two grappled, until the captain picked up a shovel and killed the German, beating him nearly to a jelly."[60]

In this pre–labor law era when the oyster industry's influence was at its height, captains were rarely prosecuted for their crimes on the Chesapeake. "Murders are seldom punished. When a body is washed ashore it is hardly

Oystermen unload their catch in Baltimore harbor, 1906. *Library of Congress Collections.*

ever possible to find out what boat it comes from, for one dredger will never tell on another," stated an 1889 article. When abusive dredge boat captains did occasionally come to trial, judges would often try to make examples of them, giving them jail time and fines meant to dissuade others from similar behavior.

During the sentencing of three Baltimore oyster captains convicted of cruelty to their crew in 1889, the presiding judge chastised the offenders, "It is scandal of the human sentiment of the community and almost of necessity, results in oppression and cruelty. In severe winters such men are often returned here, frostbitten and crippled for life." He continued, "The teaching of utterly green men the duties of a dredger, the forcing out of them enough work to get back their advanced wages, puts the masters of those vessels in a position where they cease to remember that those men are fellow creatures of flesh and blood."[61]

For some of the Chesapeake's dredge boat captains, cruelty and even murder was a small price to pay for access to the vast fortune that lay waiting to be harvested on the Bay's bottom. In an 1869 report documenting the statistics of the Chesapeake oyster trade, it was estimated that one vessel equipped with dredges could harvest up to eighteen thousand bushels per nine-month season. With bushels valued at $0.55 each, a captain might reasonably expect to make $6,300.00 at oystering per year.[62] That income was usually divided three ways—one third went toward the boat's maintenance and owners, one third went to the captain and the last third was divided between the crew. In an era before income taxes and health insurance took a healthy chunk out of take-home pay, the captain's share was roughly $2,100—when compared to the average wage of $500 per year, it was one well worth making a few moral concessions for.

Common decency toward crew members was frequently disregarded in the rush to harvest the Chesapeake's white gold, but it was hardly the only scruple oystermen sacrificed. The passage of the oyster laws in 1865 that had legalized dredging had also established specific locations for tongers in shallow water, known as "county" regions, while dredgers were restricted to harvest deeper-water areas known as "state" waters. All harvesters, whether using tongs or dredges, were now required to purchase licenses if they wanted to take oysters. In response, unlicensed vessels and poaching became rampant.

These new regulations were not only unpopular in the Chesapeake, but they were also unprecedented—with a few exceptions, prior restrictions on oystering gear or areas had generally been to protect oyster populations from outside harvesting, never from the Chesapeake's own residents. Moreover, oysters had always just been there to harvest, as free as the salt-scented air rising from the marshes. Unsurprisingly, the response to all 1865 regulations was decidedly lackluster. Just three years later, the *New York Tribune* reported: "In 1867, the dredgers began to look upon the License Law with contempt, and not more than one-half of them renewed their permits. Last year the license fee was raised to $3 per ton, the Oyster Police Force organized and equipped."[63]

Oyster licenses were sources of significant revenues—even in 1867, when only half of the oyster fleet had renewed their licenses, the state still saw $23,515 in license income. But the license law had little muscle to back it up. Oyster fines were small and infrequently levied, if at all. The new 1868 Oyster Police Force might have boasted a fine title, but it was initially equipped with only one steamboat and two sailing vessels to enforce regulations throughout the entire Maryland side of the Chesapeake Bay.

Oystermen, able sailors in any weather, soon discerned that the best time to slip by the Oyster Police unseen was at night. Sails raised and illuminated only by the moon and stars, the Bay's evening oyster fleet would depart from harbors to dredge what many oystermen saw as "god's oysters." Ironically,

Oyster sloop *J.T. Leonard* dredging under sail with cloth dredging license #26. *Library of Congress Collections.*

city oystermen, so frequently godless where mustering crew was concerned, became quite moralistic as soon as the topic of oyster licenses came up. This especially held true on the Eastern Shore and on the Chesapeake islands, where social and cultural life revolved around the church. A Smith Island man, arguing that oysters should be exempt from taxation, summed up the position of many of his colleagues by quoting scripture, "Render unto Caesar, the things that are Caesar's, and unto God, the things that are God's." When it came to these newfangled harvesting regulations, for the Bay's devout Methodists and Baptists, the only laws they needed to follow were spelled out in the Good Book. Everything else was just a suggestion.

Contemporary newspapers had a romantic term for Bay oystermen who flaunted regulations and poached at will: "pirates." And for the violent conflicts that inevitably arose between the tongers and the dredgers who nightly stripped the tongers' reserved bars of oysters: the "Oyster Wars." Pete Lesher at the Chesapeake Bay Maritime Museum is well acquainted with these infamous conflicts. It's not really surprising, he explains. "It's really hard, once somebody has something, to take it away. So we've got this oyster resource that Chesapeake oystermen have access to prior to the Civil War, and granted, we're opening it to new technology after the Civil War, but there is still this sense that regulations are taking something away."

Although in reality very few regulations were established in 1865—no catch limits, no size restrictions—Lesher sees just the establishment of the county versus state waters combined with inadequate oversight as the perfect storm for an epic fight. "You've got a natural tension set up between oystermen who are tonging and oystermen who are dredging, and in the absence of enforcement, there's the temptation to do what we will. When you've got this large a group of harvesters, and such a small police force, we get to the point of open defiance and in some cases open intimidation of law enforcement. In the 1880s, the state fishery force is chased out of lower Dorchester County on the Honga River."

Dredgers versus tongers, oystermen versus the Oyster Navy—in a world where fine houses and futures were built on oyster money, conflict between these groups was bound to erupt. A general sense of anarchy was pervasive on the Chesapeake's most productive oyster grounds, from the mouth of the Chester River to the north all the way down to the Tangier Sound.

By the end of the 1860s, just four years after the new oyster legislation was passed, the nascent state Fishery Force was lobbying for more vessels and larger crews. The commander of the Oyster Navy, the handsome and bewhiskered Hunter Davidson, appealed at an 1869 legislative budget hearing, "It is impossible with my current force to police an area that ranges from Swan Point, Kent County, down to the Potomac and upriver 125 miles." Davidson's resources were woefully inadequate, he charged, in light of the character of the oystermen he was to police, and he described them as "reckless of consequences." It was industry, Davidson continued, "more like a scramble for something adrift, where the object of everyone appears to be to get as much as he can before it is lost…Oystermen are willing to risk any weather and are willing to kill to enable them to reach the handsome profits that are now being offered to them on the market."[64]

Davidson's request was honored, and the state increased his flotilla to twelve vessels, arming each one with a Hotchkiss rapid-firing gun. Immediately, Davidson set to quelling the violence between the oystermen, which, as oyster prices topped $0.45 per bushel in 1871, resulted in deaths every week. On the Choptank, tongers with crushed skulls were found chained together, while fishermen off Tangier Island pulled up the bloated, blue corpses of drowned oystermen in their nets with an alarming frequency.

Oyster War battle on Swan Point from *Frank Leslie's Illustrated Newspaper*, January 7, 1888. *Library of Congress Collections.*

The Maryland Fishery Force, enlarged by Davidson, became a familiar sight on the Chesapeake's best—and therefore most likely to spark dispute—oyster bars. Six dredgers were captured in 1871 while dredging in the bountiful Wicomico River illegally, and their captains were taken to Deal Island to be tried. Later that winter, several more dredgers were seen poaching off tonging areas, this time on the Annemessex River. In this instance, the captains did not go quietly. When the captain on the Oyster Navy vessel *Mary Compton* called over that the dredgers should prepare for boarding, the dredge boat crew aimed and fired, spraying the Oyster Navy boat with shot. Regaining his wits, James Clements, the captain of the *Mary Compton*, loaded and fired the howitzer on her bow. One dredge boat, struck at close quarters, sank rapidly. The poachers onboard were able to swim to shore, and in the meantime, the other dredge boats beat a hasty retreat. Although no dredgers were captured, the message was clear—the Oyster Navy meant business.[65]

Over the next decade from 1870 to 1880, the conflicts continued. An 1888 article from the *New York Herald* made it clear that entire tributaries had been completely dominated by lawlessness: "The oyster pirates on the Little Choptank have not only put to flight the vessels of the State navy but they have so cowed their crews that many of the men have resigned. The tongers, whose grounds are unprotected, are the greatest sufferers. Many of them who work on the river during the last fight, were shot at repeatedly and compelled to lie flat in their boats to escape the bullets."[66]

Even with the Oyster Navy stationed at the mouth of the most notorious rivers, dredgers, tongers and the State Fishery Force fought over an oyster population that was rapidly depleting. Fewer oysters meant higher stakes and more dredge captains who felt the need to trespass into the tonger's less overworked bars. The *New York Herald* indicated that there were enough poaching captains represented on the rivers that they even managed to work together as teams: "The pirates are taking no chances. They work systematically and their forces are so distributed that in case of attack they can either separate and sail away or else combine and show fight. One of their vessels is doing guard duty right at the entrance to this ground. An oyster pirate can steal at will."[67]

Gus Rice was one of the leaders of just such a band of poachers on the Chester River. Known for his rough past and his seeming lack of fear for authority, Rice, a sometimes peach-picker and always drifter, worked on the water by day and fought in barrooms at night. In the 1870s, he drew scandal for plotting to murder State Fishery Force commander Hunter Davidson, and as the 1870s turned into the 1880s, it seemed clear he had no intention of mending his ways.

During the winter of 1887, Rice oversaw a group of dredgers that worked by the light of the moon on the dark, icy waters of the Chester River. They stationed a sentinel by the river's mouth, and a lantern on the sentinel's boat was raised or lowered to signal the approach of the Oyster Navy. As Rice's

An Oyster Navy vessel approaches a flotilla of oyster pirates. *Harper's Weekly*, January 9, 1886. *Library of Congress Collections.*

band of poachers scraped the oyster bars clean, the tongers in the region felt they had no recourse but to arm themselves in retaliation. They mounted an on-shore cannon to drive away the filching bugeyes, but it was to little effect as the tongers were considerably less skilled at aiming weapons than using nippers. Rice responded by sending a raiding party ashore, who stripped the poor tonger on cannon duty of his clothing. The naked man was sent out into the winter night to spread the word that along the Chester, it was Rice's way or no way.

Although the Oyster Navy managed to capture several of Rice's flotilla, Rice himself was as slippery as an eel. In retaliation for Rice's mistaken firing on a passenger steamer, the *Corsica*, in 1888—he believed it wrongly to be an Oyster Navy vessel and terrified the women and children onboard with his gunfire—the Fishery Force dropped the hammer. It dispatched the steamer *McLane*, armed with a howitzer and policemen with Winchester rifles, to the Chester River to apprehend the band of pirates.[68] What they found was an organized resistance—Rice's vessel and eleven other dredge boats rafted up to form a drifting battalion. The raft, shielded with iron plates, erupted with gunfire as the oyster poachers rapidly moved with the current toward the *McLane*.

Though iron armor protected the dredgers from the howitzer's reports, the *McLane* itself was used as a weapon, steaming full speed ahead into the rafted boats. All hell broke loose. Crew members leapt off the wounded dredge boat *Julia H Jones* while the *McLane* stopped, changed direction and rammed again, this time into the *JC Mahoney*.[69] The captain of the *McLane* later recounted to the *New York Times*, "It was the hottest time of the fight. The dredgers, about eight boats, were pouring broadsides into us and my crew was returning the fire as fast as possible. The *Mahoney* sunk after I rammed her. The crew crawled upon my bow calling for 'God's Sake to save them. They had had enough of dredging.'"[70] As the two boats sank, the remaining dredge boats began to disperse into the gloom.

The *McLane* went on to capture two more of the scattering dredge boats, while the rest escaped into the dusky, cold coves of the Chester. Later, the Oyster Navy would discover that its hard-earned victory was tarnished. Locked inside the hold of both of the sunken dredge boats were groups of shanghaied crew, and all had drowned. Also disappointing was the failure to capture Gus Rice, who had scarpered off upriver once the conflict turned for the Oyster Navy. But overall, the Fishery Force was victorious. For the rest of that year's oyster season at least, the bars were quiet and the skirmishes quelled on the Chester River.[71]

Struggles were not isolated to the Maryland side of the Chesapeake. Indeed, the boundary between Virginia and Maryland waters was some of the most hotly disputed oystering regions in the Bay. In Maryland, it was agreed that the boundary went from the Potomac's southern shore to Smith's Point and across to the mouth of the Pocomoke River. In Virginia, an earlier agreement from 1785 was held as the rule, which gave Maryland and Virginia reciprocal rights to the Potomac River on the Western Shore and the Pocomoke River on the Eastern Shore. That made the Pocomoke Sound and its rich oystering grounds, argued Maryland dredgers, a natural extension of the Pocomoke River. Not so, retorted Virginia oystermen, who asserted that Marylanders could only harvest oysters in a restricted portion of the Sound. The argument seems petty to modern ears, but in that period, it meant a forty-square-mile section of the Chesapeake's most productive oyster beds were up for debate.[72]

In the clear, grassy waters of the disputed boundary, these "debates" looked far more like Civil War skirmishes than reasoned conversation. The states' disagreement was played out on the Tangier and Pocomoke Sounds, pitting Maryland and Virginia Oyster Navy forces against out-of-state oystermen or leaving oystermen to take the question into their own hands. A particularly violent episode broke out in the first week of September 1874. Captain Thomas Riggin was scraping for oysters in the disputed region of the Pocomoke Sounds when a Virginia oyster inspector, W.H.B. Custis, manned his canoe and pursued the "interloper." When Riggin refused to allow Custis to board and presumably confiscate his vessel, Custis fired at Riggin's canoe in close range. Job complete, Custis then sailed for port, leaving the injured man behind. The *Baltimore Sun* reported that Riggin's canoe then drifted ashore, with Riggin "weltering in blood at the mercy of the waves, insensible from the effects of buckshot in his face and breast."[73]

The ugly dispute wasn't reconciled until 1877, although multiple "official" agreements were drawn up between Maryland and Virgina's oyster forces in an attempt to find some compromise. The final decision—derided in Maryland as the "line of '77"—conceded the lion's share of the Pocomoke Sound to Virginia. This did not fully settle the matter, at least not for each state's oystermen, who continued to poach when possible, ideally over the state line. Open feuding would break out again, several times, as oyster populations began to gradually deplete. It was an inevitable temptation as the ceaseless dredging took its toll and captains began to turn their eye away from their own overworked state beds.

From a modern perspective, the period of the oyster boom is remarkably short—from 1865 until the early 1880s. It took merely twenty years to tip a vast population of teeming oyster shoals into small, low strips of oysters, dispersed along the Bay's bottom. By the 1890s, the tide began to turn. "It is a fact beyond denial to those in Virginia and Maryland that our oyster beds are becoming depleted for want of rest and protection," charged the editor of the *Washington Post*, Thomas Morrisett, in 1890. He continued, "Millions of bushels and germ are most ruthlessly destroyed yearly in the waters and Maryland by the pernicious system of dredging."[74] Later that year, Maryland passed the very first restriction on oyster harvests to date: the Cull Law. The new regulations set a minimum legal size for market oysters, requiring oystermen to "cull" or sort their catch and throw back all oysters under two and a half inches, including shells with spat attached. The hope was that this cull law would protect smaller oysters in order to allow them to reproduce and replenish the harvested beds.

The Cull Law was not enough. "Oyster Industry Failing," proclaimed a *Baltimore Sun* headline in 1901, quickly adding the disclaimer, "But It Can and Probably Will Be Revived and Greatly Increased."[75] The article, released at the beginning of the 1901 harvest season, went on to share the alarming statistics: though Baltimore packers processed 7,403,963 bushels in 1885, by 1900, that number had dropped by half—only 3,562,144 bushels were shucked and shipped. It was clear that drastic measures were necessary, but what?

For an industry whose star rose along with the gargantuan piles of oyster shells outside of the packinghouses, the future indeed was dim. "God's oysters," once of endless plenty, would need much more than a divine intervention to return to their former economic glory. The solution would be discovered but in another kind of temple—the research lab.

# Chapter 6

# YATES BARS AND BAYLOR BEDS

Not far from the main artery running through the metropolitan sprawl of Virginia Beach, Norfolk, Portsmouth and Hampton Roads is an unseen world. Low, spreading marshes on the Lynnhaven River hum with insects, and along the waterline, funny little witches' houses protrude. These are the oyster leases, whose rough towers are exposed at low tide. A close look reveals that everything solid, from grass roots to driftwood, has a ring of spat clustered around its base.

In this astonishingly fertile, cultivated environment, it seems remarkable that the success and feasibility of oyster leases could ever have been questioned. But to nineteenth-century oystermen and twentieth-century watermen from Maryland and Virginia, the idea of owning a bit of Bay bottom was foolish, unnecessary or downright threatening to their very livelihoods. Oyster leasing and bottom cultivation were not just questioned; they were ridiculed.

Unlike land farms, all neatly regimented rows of corn and soybeans, the atmosphere of the Chesapeake thrives on the constant change of wind, tide, water and organisms. Farming is largely about environmental control—the opposite of nineteenth-century oystering. Oystermen accepted hurricanes, bad seasons and deep freezes as acts of God. Their skepticism that orderly cultivation and environmental controls could supplant or improve a wild harvest was, therefore, not surprising.

# CHESAPEAKE OYSTERS

For many, that skepticism would harden, even as scientific advances lent some credence to the benefits of oyster cultivation. For decades, the response from the Bay's oyster harvesters regarding oyster leases was at best dubious, sparking political maneuvers and red tape, lobbying and rowdy protests. Ultimately, cultivation would prove the dividing issue between Maryland and Virginia as each state moved in different directions on oyster leasing.

The modern watermen's perception of oyster leasing has a long history that begins in the nineteenth century. In response to the steep decline in the oyster harvest in the 1880s and '90s, the two states sharing the Chesapeake's main stem and its once-mighty oyster beds had very different responses. Maryland reacted by establishing a byzantine series of catch limits and size and seasonal regulations and restricting harvesters to archaic methods, like dredging under sail. Virginia, on the other hand, reacted by passing legislation that allowed for oystermen to lease barren bottom in addition to a wild fishery. Through oyster relocation and spat management, they could turn a sandy, unproductive stretch into a thriving oyster bar.

The two oyster management strategies were historically a stark, invisible line drawn across the grassy oyster beds of the Pocomoke and Tangier Sounds and the Bay's main stem to Reedville. They would each greatly shape the future of Maryland and Virginia's oyster harvests, creating two different models for the Chesapeake's oyster industry. Both approaches were in reaction to the toll that great societal, technological and scientific upheavals had taken on the Chesapeake's oysters. It was in remedy that they differed. Each seeking to increase the oyster population and bolster a vital fishery, Maryland committed to the continuation of a wild harvest, while in Virginia, oyster husbandry was embraced and implemented.

Virginia's embrace of oyster cultivation was an old idea—as old as ancient Rome and embedded in the traditional culture of the British colonists who beached their shallops on the oyster-clotted shorelines of the James River. A more contemporary example could be found in the American Northeast, which had transitioned from a wild fishery in the eighteenth century as their oyster beds were depleted. In the Chesapeake, such measures had long seemed unnecessary. The Bay's soaring, abundant oyster shoals seemed immune from the ravages of human impact. The ravenous maw of the nineteenth century had proven, however, to be a formidable adversary.

Early on, some measures had been established in the 1830s allowing for modest attempts at oyster farming, known as the "One-Acre Law." Under this legislation, Maryland landowners with a property bordering small creeks could use an acre of bottom to "produce" their own shellfish crop—a

A submerged Chesapeake oyster bed. *Photo by Jay Fleming.*

An oyster midden at low tide, Eastern Neck Island. *Photo by author.*

*Above, left*: Oyster shells excavated at Jamestown archaeological site. *Photo by author.*

*Above, right*: Archaeologist Jane Cox excavates the remains on Leavy Neck. *Photo courtesy of Jane Cox.*

*Left*: Nippers, an eighteenth-century oystering tool used to harvest individual oysters, are still used by a handful of Chesapeake watermen. *Photo by Jay Fleming.*

Oyster can collection at the Chesapeake Bay Maritime Museum. *Image by author.*

Heyser's Oyster can. *Collections of the Chesapeake Bay Maritime Museum.*

Iconic Chas. Neubert "mermaid" oyster can. *Collections of the Chesapeake Bay Maritime Museum.*

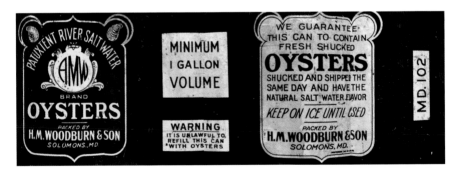

Woodburn and Son Patuxtent River Oysters can. *Collections of the Chesapeake Bay Maritime Museum.*

Baltimore Cove Oysters Trade Card. *Collections of the Chesapeake Bay Maritime Museum.*

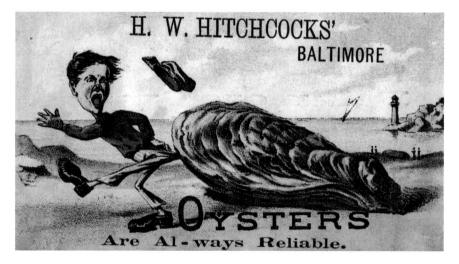

H.W. Hitchcocks' Oysters trade card. *Collections of the Chesapeake Bay Maritime Museum.*

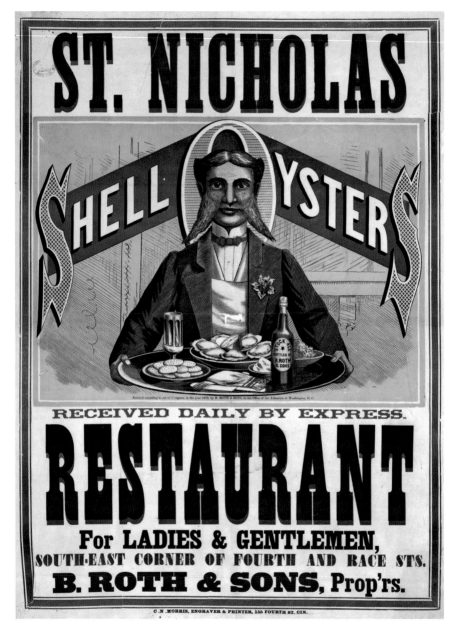

Advertisement for St. Nicholas Restaurant, whose Chesapeake oysters were supplied by train. *Library of Congress Collections.*

Skipjack *City of Crisfield* at dock, one of fewer than ten working skipjacks left in Maryland. *Photo by author.*

Postcard from Hampton, Virginia, featuring a pile of 200,000 oyster shells. *Collection of author.*

A watch house on Cedar Island. *Photo by Jay Fleming*

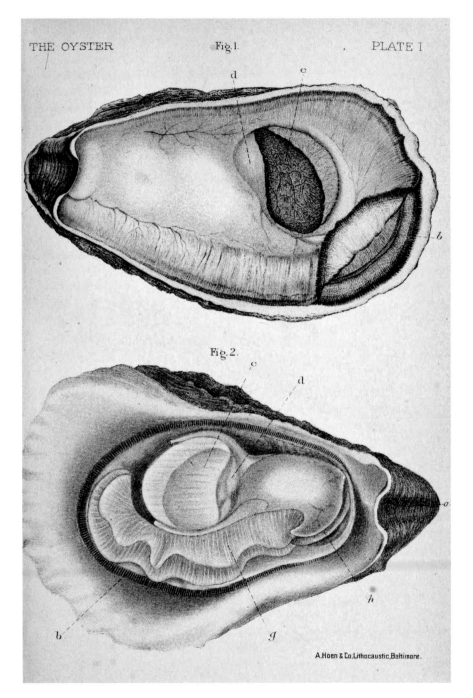

Anatomical Illustration of Eastern Oyster. *Brooks, William. The Oyster. p. 87.* © *1981, 1905, 1996 The Johns Hopkins University Press. Reprinted with permission of Johns Hopkins University Press.*

Modern-day waterman tonging for oysters. *Photo by Jay Fleming.*

Oystering fleet in the harbor at Deal Island, Maryland. *Image by author.*

Power dredging for oysters in the Tangier Sound. *Photo by Jay Fleming.*

Shucking oysters at a modern-day Chesapeake packinghouse. *Photo by Jay Fleming.*

*Left*: Power dredging vessels dockside in Wenona Harbor, Maryland. *Photo by author.*

*Below*: Tending oyster floats at the Choptank Oyster Company. *Image by author.*

*Opposite, top*: Oyster cages at Barren Island Oysters, the most popular aquaculture growing technique. *Photo by Jay Fleming.*

*Opposite, bottom*: Tumbling is a technique used to encourage a smooth aquaculture oyster with a deep cup. *Photo by Jay Fleming.*

*Left*: Barren Island oysters on a sorting belt during final quality check. *Image by author.*

*Below*: Chesapeake aquaculture oysters served on the half shell. *Photo by Jay Fleming*

*Right*: Barren Island Oyster company "BIO" oysters, boxed for shipping. *Image by author.*

*Below*: Oyster farmer Scott Budden hauls oyster cages with his father, Richard. *Image by Jennifer Deskins, courtesy of Scott Budden.*

*Robert Lee* planting Oyster Recovery Partnership oysters from Horn Point Laboratories on a sanctuary. *Photo by Jay Fleming.*

An array of aquaculture oysters from around the world at a modern oyster raw bar. *Image by author.*

move intended to replenish some of the river oyster population impacted by local tonging. The One Acre-Law also established "regions"—setting the precedent that only citizens of the contiguous county could harvest from waters within three hundred yards of shore.[76] When dredging was legalized in 1865, the legislation also allowed for up to five acres of unproductive bottom to be leased, stipulating that while productive oyster bars were off-limits, "barren" or unproductive bottom was up for grabs.

Neither initiative gained much steam. Most of the leases were located along slow-moving inland tributaries—conveniently close to home for the leaseholders but confounded by sluggish tides that failed to adequately scatter spat. But the lease locations were just the first in a series of stumbling blocks. Leaseholders also tended to be uninitiated in the proper techniques of oyster cultivation—a cultural hand-me-down that had petered out generations prior. Oyster harvesters were accustomed to gathering up wild oysters, not tending their crops like farmers. Lacking familiarity with even the basics of oyster husbandry, many oystermen just used the leased bottom as a storage location when oyster prices were low, stashing their harvests until later in the season when there was bound to be a more favorable market.

Unsurprisingly, most plots languished after a few years. Even those few leases that flourished were targets for unscrupulous oyster poachers. Ultimately, most leaseholders ended up abandoning the endeavor. They chalked up the loss not to their own inexperience but concluded that their returns were poor because oysters could only be grown on a natural, not a man-made, oyster bar. This belief would become widespread and, over time, ingrained in the traditional knowledge of oystermen. The early failures in oyster husbandry lent credence to what became a long-standing prejudice against the viability of oyster farms in the Chesapeake.

Attention was soon drawn from the small-stakes oyster lease gambles along the Bay's brackish main stem. Huge, untapped oyster shoals were discovered in the vast open waters of the Tangier and Pocomoke Sounds in the 1840s. Aided by the muscle of large schooners, efficient dredge harvesting technology legalized after the Civil War and advances in transportation, the robust wild fishery made small lease laws seem almost laughably quaint. Although a small number of leases were tended or enlarged, they were hugely overshadowed by the productivity and economy of the Bay's other oyster economy.

During the second half of the nineteenth century, Chesapeake cities exploded and the wild fishery followed. In Baltimore and Norfolk, endless rows of gritty packinghouses serviced by ceaselessly dredging skipjacks and bugeyes had turned the Chesapeake from a fertile estuary supporting a regional market into the "immense protein factory" referred to later by Baltimore author H.L. Mencken. Within a fifty-year period, the Chesapeake became a massive environmental engine powering the national seafood economy. The unceasing harvest and remarkable resilience of the Chesapeake's oyster population could not balance for long, however. In 1884, over 14 million bushels of oysters were harvested. By 1900, the catch was just over 5 million.[77] The oysters, it turns out, couldn't last forever.

Just as the Chesapeake's oyster economy was beginning to wane from its incredible apex at the end of the nineteenth century, new breakthroughs in the emerging science of biology were identifying solutions to the decline. The findings indicated that aquaculture was more than just an ancient cultural tradition. Scientific progress was another result of the Industrial Revolution, and like engineering and technology, its advances were perceived as a hallmark of a civilizing society. As the oyster harvest attenuated, the idea that one could have a better living, a better environment and a better oyster through the miracles of science would become ever more persuasive.

None was a more ardent supporter of the new methods of oyster cultivation than biologist William K. Brooks. In 1879, Brooks, a freshly minted graduate of Harvard, was one of the faculty researchers at the newly established Johns Hopkins University. Photos from the era show him to be portly and bewhiskered, with intelligent eyes peering out from a fleshy countenance. He was hardly the vision of a scientific firebrand. Looks aside, Brooks was an avid scholar who wasn't afraid to get his hands dirty in the field. He and a group of students had already spent one summer working at the mouth of the Bay, studying mussels during the inaugural year of the Chesapeake Zoological Laboratory in 1878.

In response to the worsening oyster harvests, the Maryland Fish Commission hoped to convene a similar brain trust to further science on the Chesapeake oyster. The head of the commission invited Brooks to set up another research camp the following summer in ground zero of the oyster industry—Crisfield, Maryland. Aboard a steam yacht and barges that served as floating labs, Brooks and his team of graduate students conducted unprecedented rigorous tests exploring the basic biology and reproduction of the native oyster. Thick clouds of persistent mosquitoes and oppressive humidity made for a less-than-conducive atmosphere for contemplative study, but their work was fruitful. By the summer's end, Brooks and his team of graduate students had made a groundbreaking discovery.

According to their research, Chesapeake oysters did not reproduce internally like mammals but were external reproducers like many fish species. Eggs and sperm were broadcast into the water where they mixed together and fertilized. The tiny oyster larvae were at the very bottom of the food chain, subject to the voracious appetites of predators. This type of external reproduction, while dicey for the larvae involved, was a boon to science. It meant that Brooks and other scientists might artificially create scores of larvae in labs with ease. Raised to their spat stage, these proto-oysters could then be introduced to parts of the Chesapeake where the native oyster stocks were flagging.

Brooks published his findings, which drew some scientific attention. "It (the Chesapeake oyster) refuses to be tied to its mother's apron strings," one report rather breathlessly concluded.[78] The state of Maryland was also impressed, inviting Brooks to head up a newly established Oyster Commission to investigate concerns about the impact of oyster overharvesting. Brooks would go on in the 1880s to write numerous reports on his work with the Maryland Oyster Commission, endorsing size limits, seasonal harvesting restrictions and, most controversially, aquaculture, as a way to replenish the native oyster populations. The general public, however, largely paid little heed to Brooks's discoveries or recommendations. To reach an audience beyond the boundaries of academic influence, he needed something more palatable to the nineteenth-century armchair scientist, with their books of pressed ferns and curio cabinets of fossils and shells.

Brooks had a lofty goal: to publically promote scientific aquaculture as the savior of the Chesapeake's struggling oyster population and shellfish industry. In order to fulfill his mission, Brooks wrote a book in 1891, *The Oyster*. Written in accessible language meant to appeal to the layperson, it was full of hand-drawn scientific illustrations (Brooks was an accomplished draftsman) and basic technical information about the biology, history and life cycle of the Chesapeake oyster.

In the foreword of *The Oyster*, Johns Hopkins University president Daniel Gilman summarized Brooks's pitch for oyster aquaculture, painting a picture of the mounting concerns within the state regarding the oyster industry: "After many years of plenty, Maryland is in danger of an oyster famine. Authentic figures showing the decline and fall of the oyster empire of the Chesapeake startle all who consider them…The author has another claim to be heard: [emphasis in original] THE DEMAND FOR CHESAPEAKE OYSTERS HAS OUTGROWN THE NATURAL SUPPLY…The remedy he proposes is to increase the supply by artificial means."

Brooks's experiments proved that *Crassostrea virginica* could propagate in open water. As opposed to the European oyster, *Crassostrea edulis,* which had to be artificially reproduced inside the female oyster's shell in a tedious process, the ease of lab-producing a healthy spat set for Chesapeake oysters was seen by Brooks as an enormous biological asset. Mother Nature just needed a bit of a boost in the Bay. The roadblocks were cultural and legislative, rather than environmental. "All that is needed," stated Brooks in *The Oyster*, "in order to make this great source of wealth available to our people, is the permission to enter oyster culture. When the citizens of Maryland demand the right to enter into this new industry, and to reclaim their property that is now going to waste, a new era of prosperity will be introduced and the oyster area will be developed with great rapidity."

In *The Oyster*, Brooks supported his position with the results of his science experiments and observations, many of which have become standards of today's oyster industry. For instance, his conclusion that the Bay's oyster beds were founded on ancient layers of fossilized oyster shells is now commonly accepted. He also relied on global best practices to support his position. In *The Oyster*, Brooks cited both recent examples as well as ancient historic texts that highlighted the aquaculture successes of other countries, cultures and regions. The cultivation techniques of ancient Rome, as well as eighteenth-century France and nineteenth-century New England were examined and theoretically applied to the Chesapeake.

Today's environmentalists view oysters and a shift toward cultivation as an essential part of the solution for the troubled water quality of the Chesapeake. However, Brooks felt that oysters (and therefore oyster cultivation) were important because of their critical role in the Bay's economy. "Oyster farming will provide permanent, stable employment for our oystermen, it will increase the packing business, it will benefit all oyster dealers, all shuckers and can makers, it will provide cheap and abundant food for our people, and it will contribute to the revenues of the State."

Brooks's belief in the importance of oysters to the Chesapeake was absolute. During his decades of studying Chesapeake shellfish, it also seemed to have become a bit of an obsession. Famously taciturn, Brooks was nicknamed "Mummy" during his school days, and was a notoriously bad guest at university social events. At one reception, Brooks gamely attempted to make small talk with a society woman. He allowed her to go on for a while, seemingly preoccupied. Finally, after excruciatingly enduring her small talk for as long as he was able, Brooks burst out, "Madam, the Maryland oyster is being exterminated!"[79]

Brooks was not alone in his assessment that the troubled Chesapeake oyster population was in need of some radical intervention—especially if the hundreds of thousands of Maryland residents involved in the oyster industry were to keep their jobs. By the publication of *The Oyster*, Maryland was among thirty states with fishery agencies, following the establishment in 1871 of the National U.S. Fish Commission. Both national and state organizations sought to apply the best agricultural practices developed for farming to the fisheries. Their goal was lofty, hoping not only to sustain the fishing-related industries in their region but also that it was possible to "achieve a moral balance between nature and culture." It was with this idealistically progressive bent that Brooks and his students convened in Crisfield in 1879 and which would compel Brooks's decade of oyster research.

There were other attempts by the state of Maryland to triage the Chesapeake oyster population besides Brooks's work. A commission charged by the Maryland General Assembly oversaw work in 1878 and 1879 by Lieutenant Francis Winslow of the U.S. Coast and Geodetic Survey to map the Chesapeake's remaining oyster bars. In response to accusations of over-dredging, the survey was intended to provide a baseline, tallying the oyster's productiveness, boundaries and ability to recover from the harsh teeth of dredges and environmental punishment. It didn't end on optimistic findings—the survey's report stated that oysters could no longer keep up with the pace of current harvests. However, the report identified remedies for the replenishment of overharvested beds, including some cultivation techniques.

Dredging, Winslow's report concluded, was not all bad for the oysters. In fact, the harvesting techniques had broken up the natural reef structures, spreading out the boundaries of the natural beds. These enlarged oyster bars provided individual oysters with less competition for space and resources, producing larger, healthier specimens. The broadened oyster bars, with the distributed base of old oyster shells, or "cultch," also created a foundation for a healthy spat set. But without a sustainable population of mature oysters, no spat would be produced to cover these expanded oyster bars with a new generation of oysters.

This, Winslow's report suggested, could be remediated through cultivation techniques—old beds could be beefed up with rocks, broken earthenware and reused oyster shells from shucking houses and then seeded with mature oysters. But for the oyster population to truly reestablish itself, sweeping oversight was recommended. To address the overharvesting, the report continued, a partisan oyster commission should be established to oversee the fishery. Oyster grounds rich with young oysters should be protected from harvest. A closed season should be established during the oysters' summer spawning period.

These recommendations of Winslow's survey report would be repeated by subsequent studies and commissions conducted in the following decade to address the continually declining oyster harvests. Some even went further, endorsing a system of private oyster cultivation beyond the limited leases available to waterfront landowners, based upon the New England model. Many, like closed oystering seasons, replacement of shell cultch and the seeding of public beds with spat, are now familiar as the backbone of modern regulations in the Chesapeake. At the time, their common-sense suggestions—though supported by science and endorsed by the state government—were not universally embraced.

Many who profited from the current oyster industry, especially individual harvesters, distrusted aquaculture and particularly private oyster farms. Oyster cultivation was perceived as the realm of science, which then, as now, is often met with suspicion in the Chesapeake. Brooks and his colleagues were seen as lab scientists, gentlemen scholars, and their prescribed solutions for the oyster populations often ran contrary to the native knowledge of the working class oystermen. In 1905, Brooks commented, "I speak on this subject with the diffidence of one who has been frequently snubbed and repressed…so I have learned to be submissive in the presence of the elderly gentleman who studied the embryology of the oyster when years ago as a boy he visited his grandfather on the Eastern Shore, and to listen with deference to the shucker as he demonstrates to me at his raw-box, by the aid of his hammer and shucking-knife, the fallacy of my notions of the structure of the animal."[80]

Brooks was challenged in public, too. At a rally in the train track–laced neighborhood of Camden, in Baltimore in 1891, a crowd turned out to criticize his work and other proponents of oyster cultivation. "Professor Brooks says the failure in supply does not result from the methods of taking, nor the seasons, but from an inexhaustible demand," commented speaker Colonel Henry Page, continuing, "a natural bed only needs protection."

Other speakers expressed skepticism regarding the dire predictions leveled at the future of the Chesapeake oyster population: "An industry which gives employment to upward of 55,000 people, and indirectly contributes to the support of 220,000 more, which keeps 8,800 boats working in our oyster fisheries, and which yielded 9,650,000 bushels of edible oysters to the pack last season, is suddenly going to dry up and die out unless 'professor' steps in and lends the helping hand of science to old Dame Nature."[81]

A distrust for technology, an undercurrent borne of the rapid changes eddying from the booming industrial age, was another concern addressed at the rally: "The loss of the free fishery would destroy thousands of jobs by replacing watermen with steam-powered dredges thereby plunging the tidewater into an eclipse which this generation will not see lightened."[82]

The resistance to oyster cultivation by oystermen stemmed from a few central concerns, many highlighted in the Camden rally. Firstly, Maryland oyster beds should belong to and be harvested by Marylanders only—no "foreign" interference from New England was acceptable (though actual foreigners in the packinghouses were another story). Secondly, corporate interests should not be allowed to monopolize the oyster beds, and the oyster economy should be based on individuals rather than big businesses. And finally, oystermen believed that oysters could only be grown on a natural, rather than artificial, oyster bar. By their argument, this meant that leasing could only take place on natural oyster bars—which should not be subject to private harvests.

The nineteenth-century American economy ground tirelessly on a system of private interests that impacted every level of society. Chesapeake oysters were no exception. From a single tonger on a quiet bar to the prosperous railroad magnates in glossy black suits, oysters represented a substantial source of income. Oysters were money—and that money represented power. For the oyster harvesters, distrustful of state and private interference, loss of a free oyster harvest represented, at best, marginalization and, at worst, infringement on their basic rights.

To protect the common oyster harvest, nineteenth- and early twentieth-century oystermen had other tools at their disposal than just barbed words and waterfront rallies—they could vote. The majority of Maryland's counties were located adjacent to waterfront, thus giving them a disproportional stake in maintaining the oyster industry's power. Combined with a state representational allotment that gave rural counties as much voting power as more populous ones, oystermen were able to manipulate oyster legislation through the legal political system. In addition, major industries like railroads and packinghouses provided the persuasive financial influence to grease the oystermen's squeaky political wheel.

These combined economic forces with an unstoppable political will were known as the "oyster vote." A *Washington Post* article explained in 1905 that the oyster vote was "made up of those fishermen, dredgers, boatmen, packers, and sorters who vote in the counties of Maryland which are on or near Chesapeake Bay or the Potomac River or their tributaries." It continued, "There are twenty-four counties in Maryland of which twenty are on the Chesapeake, the Potomac, or the Atlantic Ocean. Under these circumstances, the oyster vote is often decisive and it is the custom of both political parties to adopt at their conventions an oyster plank favorable to the demands of those whose livelihood comes from the oyster business."[83]

By contrast, in Virginia, most rural counties were not located in the Tidewater—therefore fishermen in the Chesapeake's southernmost state didn't enjoy the same political clout as their northern counterparts. There, in the salt-stained cordgrass marshes, marginal influence meant the oystermen's traditions were vulnerable to the wheels of political, economic and scientific change.

The power of the Maryland oystermen's vote was tested a few years later in the early 1900s, when Baltimore attorney and legislator Howard Haman began lobbying to pass the Haman Oyster Culture Act. The proposed legislation would permit leases up to ten acres in county waters and one hundred acres in the Tangier Sounds, and in the Bay's main stem, leases up to five hundred acres were allowed. To appease the fishermen and their concerns about corporate competition, the Haman Act restricted one lease per person to Maryland leaseholders only, and leasers were required to only harvest with tongs rather than dredges so as not to compete directly with oystermen harvesting a wild catch.

The Haman act was wildly divisive, and editorials in Chesapeake newspapers illustrated the heated emotions on both sides of the "oyster question." In early statements, Haman welcomed debate of his controversial proposal: "We want this proposition criticized. We invite debate and solicit intelligent examination and investigation of the plan we propose." He continued, "The greatest natural supply of oysters in the world existed at one time in the Chesapeake Bay. This supply has been wasted and thrown away in the most negligent and reckless manner, until now all classes of people who depend for a living upon the vast packing business of Maryland are threatened with the loss of that living at no distant date. The entire canned goods industry will be destroyed."[84]

Haman asked for debate, and he got it. In public forums and in column after column of newsprint, the Haman Act was excoriated. In an editorial in *The American* on March 4 1901, an Easton, Maryland oysterman, John Burt, laid out the case against Haman's proposal:

> *The Haman Bill has many alluring features, but to the oysterman it does not hold out many inducements. They see that their livelihood would*

> *gradually be curtailed, that they would be forced to abandon all hope of making an honest living…The oyster grounds would be leased almost exclusively to the landowners and capitalists. Let the State of Maryland appropriate sufficient money to properly shell the bottom of the Chesapeake. The oystermen would benefit by that greatly. There is no class of people more deserving of aid in that direction than the oystermen.*

Burt's plea that the State of Maryland establish initiatives to directly aid oystermen through the dispersal of shell was amazingly prescient. Even now, watermen appeal to improve existing oyster bars rather than artificially creating new ones. Timeless, too, is the argument that leasing efforts (promoted by Haman and many since) will only open the Bay's bottom up to corporate rather than individual interests. Burt's contemporaries were also concerned about the depressing impact private production of oysters might have on the market price of wild harvested oysters—when oysters were already so cheap, a new flood of oysters, they feared, would significantly harm their profits.[85]

Editorials in Virginia and Maryland newspapers, however, indicated increasing frustration over the oystermen's staunch position on wild harvesting. In an opinion piece in the *Baltimore American* entitled, "The Truth Which Hurts," it is clear that the protests had not won over every Chesapeake resident:

> *Year after year it has been pointed out that planting on a large scale and by a well-regulated method will alone save the oyster, and yet every time this is recommended a protest comes from the oystermen, who declare that oyster-planting would ruin their business and take bread from their mouths. Maryland has heeded these absurd requests, and as a result its oyster business grows less every year. The moral is plain, but oystermen will not heed it.[86]*

This view was widespread enough to carry the Haman Act into law in 1906, to the great consternation of the oystermen. Next steps were undertaken to map the bottom of the Chesapeake so that lease plots might be drawn. Brooks and his acolytes appeared to have triumphed—but in a state tangled up in oyster money and oyster interests, a long-term divergence from traditional harvesting would prove to be exceedingly difficult to maintain.

In order to establish the boundaries of the extensive new leases and to delineate existing oyster beds, a newly created Shellfish Commission began a survey from 1906 to 1912 of the natural oyster bars in state waters. The surveys were undertaken by a Captain C.C. Yates, who used a team of crew members and multiple vessels of various sizes and draughts to explore every oyster bed, from the most shallow to the deep channel reefs. Designated productive natural bars were classified by size, oyster density and bottom type and were charted in polygons on the survey maps. The survey and its 779 "Yates bars" would ultimately become an essential document of both the oyster industry and the future environmental movement. Its maps, documenting the existing oyster bars of the nineteenth-century Chesapeake, would one day be critical information for watermen and conservationists as they sought to restore the vanished reefs of the Bay's bottom.

The contemporary response to the Yates survey by Maryland's oystermen, however, was decidedly underwhelming. They felt that mapping was a fruitless endeavor and dismissed the survey as irrelevant. In their view, the natural boundaries of oyster bars could shift depending on the season, acts of god or natural spat set. No amount of mapping could ever pin the organic structure of oyster reefs to the Bay's bottom—they were living things. The oystermen furthermore concluded that efforts to transform barren bottom into oyster beds through plantings of spat and seed were patently useless, as they were products of Mother Nature. In a letter to the editor of the *Baltimore American* in February 1909, an oysterman from the working waterfront town of Solomons wrote, "We, as oystermen along the tidewater counties, believe that the next legislature will abolish this nuisance [the Haman Act] and compel the gentlemen who are drawing their fat salaries…to relieve the State of Maryland of a great responsibility, for as any practical oysterman knows, where oysters do not grow naturally you cannot make them grow, by wasting shells and seed oysters."

With this sentiment in mind, the oystermen used their political might to strip the Haman Act with a subsequent bill in 1914, the Shepherd Act. The Shepherd Act reformed the restrictions of the Haman Act with regulations that undermined leasing on the word of the traditional oyster harvesters. It stated that any barren grounds that had been harvested by an oysterman in the prior five years were to be reclassified as a Yates bar and therefore restricted from leasing. All an oysterman needed to do if he objected to a new lease was file a claim stating that on one day in the previous five years, he had caught oysters on that spot. With the Shepherd Act in place, the courts generally ruled in the favor of the claimant, with no further corroboration necessary other than the testimony of an individual fisherman. In this fashion, from 1915 to 1963, fifteen thousand nonproductive acres of lease-ready bottom were transformed on paper to thriving, off-limits oyster reefs.[87]

Only a few outliers were established in this anti-cultivation Maryland atmosphere, and some even managed to establish substantial leasing businesses. J.C. Lore and Sons in Solomons was one of the largest oyster growers on the Western Shore of Maryland that managed to thrive despite the restrictions. On the Eastern Shore, the H.B. Kennerly Company in the town of Nanticoke along the Nanticoke River encouraged a sizeable community of leaseholders. After the passing of the Haman Oyster Culture Law, the packinghouse and seafood distributors encouraged local watermen to obtain leases so they might grow oysters for Kennerly to process. In return, the H.B. Kennerly Company provided shell cultch from their packinghouse for leaseholders to use on their individual oyster beds.[88]

The Nanticoke's wild spat set was so prolific that no additional seeding was necessary, and the leases prospered on the river's mighty fertility. The system worked well for the packinghouse, enabling it to pack shellfish all year long, and for the watermen, it provided an easy stop-gap between the end of the public oyster season and the start of the summer crabbing harvest. For two generations, this remarkable little cluster of leases proliferated in the easy curve of the Nanticoke, an island of productive oyster cultivation in a Bay full of protest.

While Maryland wavered for decades on whether to embrace oyster cultivation and how much, Virginia's position was much less hesitant. In 1892, in response to the same crash in oyster harvests that had produced such economic angst in Maryland, Virginia initiated its own survey of the existing natural oyster beds. These, known as "Baylor Beds" in reference to the surveyor, Lieutenant James B. Baylor, were off-limits for leases. Everything else, about 251,050 acres, was designated "barren" and was opened to the public for leasing. Not everyone loved this concept, including the Virginia Oysterman's Protective Association, which argued that "proprietary rights in oyster beds will make men who may now at any time place their tongs in their boats and labor when they will, will be driven from the business. They will make a strong fight for their rights, as against those of a monopoly."[89]

These entreaties to maintain the status quo did little to effect change. Virginia, which already had representation at the state level far less friendly to wild oystering interests, moved forward with its legislation. Subsequently, Virginia closed any loopholes in the legislation that would have allowed for legal challenges the way Maryland's Shepherd Act did.

In the next few decades in Virginia, additional laws were passed to fortify leaseholder's rights, with the passage in 1910 of a law allowing leasing rights for corporations. With little fuss, the welcome mat was rolled out for Virginia oyster farms. Quickly, private grounds became the source of over half of Virginia's overall oyster harvest, with the commonwealth eclipsing Maryland's status as the largest oyster-producing state in the Chesapeake. A *Washington Post* article in 1895 exulted, "Gourmands need not fear that the delicacy will ever become extinct." It continued, painting a picture of an orderly system: "To the novice, it is a matter of wonder how the skipper can sail into his own particular garden every morning. The frail stakes protect the owner from intrusion as securely as if his garden were surrounded by a stone wall. This is all part of the morality of the oystermen."[90]

While the journalist from the *Washington Post* may have observed oyster farmers on their best behavior, the simultaneous establishment of "watch towers" tells a different story. As oyster leases grew, the expansion of the industry could be observed by the erection of these small shacks, built over oyster leases on pilings. Replete with kitchens, beds and other homely comforts, watch houses allowed leaseholders to live directly over their oyster beds, discouraging poachers—often Maryland oystermen who trespassed across state lines. Spindly watch houses proliferated throughout the Tidewater's low marshes along with the oyster farms. For eighty years, they were as much part of the landscape as the red-billed oystercatchers that squabbled among the spat.

The division between the oyster industries of the two states only grew during the twentieth century. In Virginia, leasing continued to expand and prosper, with 48,000 acres leased by 1900 and 134,000 acres by the peak year, in 1967.[91] Across the state line, Maryland's oystermen continued to solidify their stance against proposed leasing programs, using their political clout to influence the lawmakers in Annapolis as well as vocalizing their objections publicly in newspapers, petitions and rallies. They had some key opportunities to flex their collective muscle, notably in 1927.

In response to a bill proposing a sweeping expansion of leasing regulations made by Governor Albert Ritchie, oystermen, oystermen's associations and lobbyists unified, firing on the proposal in public forums, rallies and in the press. An oysterman, Captain Alfred Moss, reflected the broad views of the oyster industry when he railed against the proposal that year in the *Baltimore Sun*: "Is it fair to take our oyster rock away from us? That's all right for capitalists, the fellows who own the packing houses [*sic*] and have a lot of money to plant leased beds, but what are the dredgers and the tongers going to do if all that bottom is taken away from them?" The public outcry and political maneuvering that followed ultimately killed the bill. The governor,

A leaseholder keeps watch at a Virginia oyster watch house in Tom's Cove. Photo by A. Aubrey Bodine. *Courtesy of the Mariner's Museum, Newport News, Virginia.*

under heavy political pressure, abandoned his unpopular position on the proposal. He had learned his lesson. During Ritchie's final years in office, the idea of leasing was never broached again.

Throughout the twentieth century, successive efforts were made to turn Maryland's common fishery into a privatized one, but the sallies of the pro-leasing lobby met with continual resistance from Maryland oystermen. Though the Chesapeake oyster industry suffered from a downturn during the Depression along with the rest of the American economy, from the 1930s until the 1960s, the harvest was relatively steady. State regulations on oystering seasons, gear and catch limits seemed enough to maintain the oyster population—weakening the argument for introducing leasing as a remedy for overharvesting. While the wild excesses of the 1880s oyster boom might never again return, it seemed that oysters were secure in their place as the winter cornerstone catch.

It was during this era in the early twentieth century that the concept of "oystermen" ceased to exist. It was replaced by the concept of multi-season "watermen" for whom oysters were just one of the big three harvests, along with fish and crabs. As the oyster population attenuated in the post-boom era, the entire industry was forced to reconfigure and adapt. Some waterfront towns, like St. Michaels, Crisfield and Solomons, that had been almost solely built around oyster harvesting, packing and shipping now saw blue crab packinghouses taking the place of shuttered oyster processors.

The Chesapeake's fishermen transitioned as well, becoming seasonal harvesters of several catches—oysters, crabs and finfish—as they became available, rather than cleaving to one lucrative single harvest. Although "waterman" is a traditional old English term, it is this twentieth-century iteration—the independent Chesapeake fisherman chasing a seasonal harvest—that is what we know today.

In theory, with the equilibrium reached between oyster populations, diversified seasonal harvests and harvesting regulations, the traditional Chesapeake wild oyster fishery in Maryland might well have continued to the modern day. But the twentieth century held great, unforeseen changes for the Chesapeake and its oyster populations. The Bay's unspoiled beauty and thriving fisheries, seemingly perpetual, were really quite fragile after all.

# CHAPTER 7

# SANCTUARY, CONTROVERSY

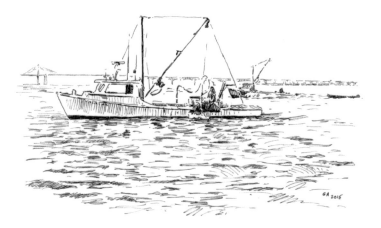

On an overcast morning in late April 2014, the mouth of the Little Choptank River is glassy and still—what Eastern Shoremen refer to as "slick calm." This small tributary, just south of the greater Choptank River, is a place of shallow water and dense marshes. Traditionally, it has also been one of the most productive oyster regions in the Chesapeake. During the time of the Oyster Wars, some of the most raucous, violent conflicts were here. Since then, it's been mostly quiet, worked by oystering watermen over the decades of plenty and the ones of low harvest and disease.

Today, the peace of a century has been broken. A barge, piled high with Florida-sourced fossilized cultch, is headed upriver, to be washed overboard and used to build up the Little Choptank's bottom to encourage a healthy spat set. Before the barge is a line of workboats, white on the silver water. These are the vessels of protesting watermen, here to object to the shell and the fine silt that laces it. It will cover crabs, they argue, and it is too fouled by clay to encourage a good spat set. In some ways, the watermen protest out of hope—that in the not-too-distant future, they will again be able to harvest oysters here. Right now, that is illegal. The Little Choptank, in its entirety, is now an oyster sanctuary.

This standoff reflects the changes oysters, watermen and the Chesapeake Bay have undergone over the last fifty years. Oyster diseases from the 1960s onward devastated not only a fishery but also a vital environmental keystone species whose importance scientists were just beginning to appreciate. Simultaneously, the water quality in the Chesapeake began to buckle under the pressure of rapidly expanding cities, suburbs, highways and high-yield farms. The Chesapeake, once clear, with magnificent oyster shoals, became the modern Bay we worry about. Turbid and soupy with algae, the Bay now struggles to support life.

Oysters have become part of the remedy—filtering water, supporting aquatic life and slowing wave action so bottom grasses can thrive. Once valued only as a food, oysters are now considered a panacea for the environmental ills troubling the Chesapeake. But the future for oysters, as a fishery and as an ecological remedy, is unclear. Oysters continue to be a point of controversy, as the wild oystering industry clashes with new environmental regulations limiting oyster harvests and establishing oyster sanctuaries. This standoff on the Little Choptank is about more than cultch. It is a conflict over the sustainability of a common fishery in an environmentally imperiled estuary, the role of science and that of a deeply rooted Chesapeake culture. These are the new Oyster Wars. Fought in words, in legislation and sometimes in protest, they are evidence of the oyster's enduring legacy in the Bay's environment, economy and identity.

In the early part of the twentieth century following the oyster boom years, the oyster harvest continued to decline and then gradually leveled out in the decades from 1930 to 1980—ranging annually between 2 and 4 million bushels per year in Maryland and 4 and 6 million bushels per year for Virginia.[92] While Maryland and Virginia deliberated the merits of oyster cultivation and moved into two different directions, wild oyster harvesters found what seemed to be a sustainable stride. Sailing out from Chesapeake harbors to harvest oysters in the cold months, watermen had transitioned from one-catch "oystermen" into the modern, multi-seasonal occupation their name now connotes. Although many packinghouses had shuttered as the salad days of the oystering business had concluded, a core still remained, canning and packing crabs in the summer and oysters in the winter in Crisfield, Solomons, St. Michaels and Baltimore.

The watermen's tools continued to adapt as time advanced, especially their boats. Two-sail bateaux—or as they're commonly known, "skipjacks"—with generous decks and low draft were the new iteration of oyster vessels. They were constructed not of logs like bugeyes but using entirely new techniques. This aspect of their design took advantage of newly cheap and abundant milled lumber and allowed skipjacks to be built much more rapidly than their log-built predecessors.[93]

Like bugeyes, the skipjack's whimsical name appeared without an obvious origin—some have suggested it comes from old English or because of its resemblance to skipjack mackerel. Wherever the term started, it quickly became synonymous with a forty- to fifty-foot workhorse, propelled by sail and loaded low to the water with enormous piles of oysters. These powerful vessels could pull two dredges at a time and had deck capacity to carry up to five hundred bushels of oysters. Eventually, some of them even had engines installed in small "pushboats"—attached dinghies that provided power without taking up valuable real estate in the skipjack's hull. Skipjacks, rawboned working ladies named after daughters or mothers, often dredged in proximity as a fleet. Cresting the Chesapeake's brackish waves, their sails extended, the skipjack fleet at work looked like a cloud of egrets, graceful and rapacious. By the early twentieth century, they were the oystering boat of choice, and the fleet had swelled to two thousand vessels in size.

Skipjacks were not the only thing proliferating. Population in the Chesapeake continued to grow as the nineteenth century turned into the twentieth. In 1880, 330,000 residents called Baltimore home, and by 1910, that figure had swelled to 560,000 people.[94] Similar development was taking place in Washington, D.C., and Norfolk, Virginia, as government, shipping and naval forces grew. The Chesapeake's infrastructure was ill equipped to handle these new urban populations. At the turn of the century, not a single Chesapeake city had a sewer system.

Baltimore relied solely on eighty thousand privy vaults to address the problem that merely slowed the waste before it eventually ended up in the Patapsco River. Although Baltimore invested in other projects typical of the Progressive Era—urban parks and street paving—it was clear that the old model of thinking about the Bay hadn't changed. The Chesapeake could be simultaneously considered a cornucopia of plenty and an appropriate receptacle for sewage, industrial chemicals and household trash.

This system or lack thereof was clearly problematic. Baltimore's stench "is a 2000-horse-power smell that lays Limburger cheese in the shade," described an editorial in July 1897. The harbor, where once fishermen pulled seine nets, more closely resembled a toilet than a thriving estuary: "The water of the basin is simply filthy, and instead of being clear water is an opaque body of sewerage. It can be smelled blocks away when stirred up by the constantly moving steamers. The passengers on the excursion steamers get the full benefit of this stench, and those who have been down the bay previously this season, carry handkerchiefs well saturated with cologne which they hold to their noses from the time they leave Light-street wharf until they get outside the harbor."[95]

Besides the unpleasant atmosphere and smells produced by Baltimore's open gutters, such careless disregard of effluent could have deadly consequences. Typhoid and cholera epidemics in the late nineteenth century had their origins in inadequate or nonexistent waste facilities, and the deaths and public outcry it caused spurred municipalities to action.[96] In 1912, a typhoid outbreak in New York City and Chicago was eventually traced to a batch of tainted oysters, provoking widespread outrage and an overall drop in national oyster sales. Baltimore's still-mighty "oyster vote" was rightfully alarmed. How the Bay's shellfish industry had managed to avoid such a devastating epidemic up until that point was just sheer luck. Watermen worked in the Patapsco and farther south harvesting oysters, and millions of these organisms were undoubtedly filtering plenty of Baltimore's slightly diluted filth—only hours before being shucked, packed and shipped out to points across the country.

The city was well primed for a public works water treatment project on a large scale. The Great Fire of 1904 had leveled most of Baltimore's industrial neighborhoods. Galvanized by the crisis, the city planners addressed the sewage issue with strong encouragement by oyster stakeholders. Under pressure from oyster businesses that vociferously objected to some suggestions that "dilution was the solution," a bill was passed ensuring that only treated sewage "pronounced to be free from all impurities detrimental to the oyster or fish industry" was allowed to drain into the Chesapeake Bay.[97]

Watermen, oyster packers and seafood shippers all breathed a sigh of relief. Although tainted oysters would continue to make headlines into the twentieth century, with Baltimore's effluent under control, they wouldn't be traced back to the Bay's oyster beds. By addressing its unpleasant and dangerous outflow problem, Baltimore not only eliminated its Limburger smell, but it also passed the first truly environmental legislation in the Chesapeake Bay.

In order to calm customers, oyster packers promoted the cleanliness and purity of their product on their oyster cans. Heyser's Oysters, packed by the Wm. Heyser Company in Baltimore, boasted the guarantee that "oysters contained in this can were packed in the most advanced sanitary manner to meet the requirements of the pure food regulations." The buxom mermaid decorating the WH Killian Company's "Sea-L-Tite Oysters" now shared space with a lengthy assurance that "Sea-L-Tite Oysters are selected natural growth oysters from deep salt water beds. All that is naturally good—flavor, nutriment, vitamines [sic] fresh life elements sealed right in this container just as they came from the shell. All usable—no waste—more net ounces of wholesome food for the money than in any flesh food."

These effusive pledges of cleanliness and sanitation reflected a greater national interest in food safety. Upton Sinclair's 1907 labor exposé, *The Jungle*, had intended to awaken the American public to the injustices suffered by industrial workers. Instead, as Sinclair would later state, his gory descriptions of Chicago's meat packing industry had an unintended effect: "I aimed at the public's heart, and by accident I hit it in the stomach." *The Jungle* and the resulting public backlash against the stomach-turning conditions of industrial food production would have a sweeping impact. Outraged readers inundated President Theodore Roosevelt with letters demanding action—ultimately resulting in the passage of the Food and Drug Act. Food contamination was high in public consciousness—something that intensified the waves of panic throughout the Chesapeake's oyster producers during the typhoid scare of 1912. For the first time, they realized, the oysters they sold and the health of the Bay were inextricably intertwined.

What Chesapeake residents didn't understand, however, was the vital role oysters played in maintaining the Bay's cleanliness and water quality. The Chesapeake estuary was so immense that even environmental disasters like that represented in Baltimore's harbor tended to be highly localized. Once away from the immediate area, the effluent or runoff was diffused by the Bay's vast volume of tidal water. Oyster bars, menhaden schools, submerged bay grasses and marshes worked to remediate the remaining algae, nutrients and sediment that the Chesapeake's growing population produced. Throughout the early twentieth century, these natural filters of the Chesapeake Bay were balanced on a thin knife's edge. As oysters were harvested, farms increased their yield and communities expanded, the pressure on the Chesapeake's environment only magnified.

The great world wars of the twentieth century were the only early interruptions to the steady harvest of Chesapeake oysters. Young, hale watermen left their boats at the dock and headed for the theaters of war in France and Germany and, later, Italy, Japan and the Pacific. What those who returned several years later discovered was an oyster renaissance—in the watermen's absence, the Chesapeake's oyster bars had flourished. The watermen lost no time getting back to work. New skipjacks were commissioned to meet the demand, and their skeletal forms shed sawdust and caulking as, side by side, a fleet emerged from piles of lumber.

The wild harvest was supplemented in this period by a series of initiatives that aimed to boost the natural production of spat in in marginal areas. These were inspired by the research of Dr. R.V. Truitt, who had transplanted oysters from the low-salinity reaches of the Upper Bay and experimented

A revitalized post–World War II skipjack fleet. Photo by HR Hollyday. *Courtesy of Talbot County Historical Society.*

with ways to encourage spat settlement. Truitt's work—largely common sense—confirmed the importance of "spent" oyster shell as a landing material for larval spat and the positive relationship between a high mature population of breeding oysters and an increase in the quantity of larval spat. In short, he concluded, oysters want to grow on other oysters, and the more mature oysters you retain, the more babies are produced. Unlike W.K. Brooks, who had strongly advocated for oyster cultivation, Truitt did not verge into the political fray—a fact that helped to advance his recommendations in Annapolis. In 1927, based on his research, laws were passed that required oysters to reach at least three inches to be considered "legal size"—thus ensuring their ability to reproduce—and requiring the return of shell and brood oysters to beds needing improvement.[98]

Along with the legislation encouraged by Truitt's work, several other conservation measures were passed in the Maryland legislature in 1927. A shell-planting program was undertaken, financed by a combination of appropriations, a two-cents-per-bushel oyster tax and a gas tax on workboats. An additional tax was levied on packinghouses, requiring them to return 10 percent of their shell cultch to the state for planting initiatives.[99] There was even a state cultivation program established on a one-thousand-acre "reserve" area on the Honga River intended to improve overharvested beds through shell infusions. Although cultivation continued to be viewed with suspicion, this particular endeavor, designed to aid the traditional wild fishery, was deemed acceptable by the almighty oyster vote.

Truitt was encouraged by the results. The clean shells had spurred a rich spat set where nothing had grown for years and suggested the possibilities of a well-managed fishery. The Honga River's newly restored oyster bar didn't last long, however. The reserve area, transformed into renewed productivity by the layers of new oyster shell, was summarily turned back over to the public for use as a tonging site. But the significance of Truitt's reserve area would indeed have long-lasting effects. Seed-production programs and shell conservation would become part of Maryland's recipe for the sustainability of the wild oyster harvest, lauded by watermen to the current day as a crucial component of the last good period of oystering on the Chesapeake.

In the 1950s, the importance of sources of shell were reiterated in new laws that required oyster packers to return 50 percent of their spent shell back to the state. Where that shell ended up was often decided by new political entities—state and county oystermen's committees. Created by the Commission on Conservation of Natural Resources in an attempt to unify the long-divided tongers and dredgers, these committees were given a strong voice on state conservation measures, from planting seed and shell to closing oyster bars.

Watermen had long-held opinions on such matters, based on observation and a lifetime's worth of experience working the Bay's oyster beds. They also had a strong stake in continuing to support their livelihoods. But the recommendations of these county oystermen's committees often conflicted with scientific findings. Watermen chose to put shell in areas based on their recollections and gut instincts—locations that were often deemed unsuitable by scientists. They fought over the state's attempts to transport oysters from one county's productive bed to the overharvested ones over the county line. While the state's new county committees had indeed successfully unified the tongers and dredgers, the committees' new solidarity often resisted state recommendations—a resistance that would grow as regulations tightened.

Maryland's seed and shell programs—popular initiatives among watermen who directly benefited from the renewed productivity of once-struggling oyster bars—expanded as the 1960s progressed. However, the demand for supplies of oyster shell, even with a 50 percent shell tax, outstripped the supply. Maryland had to get creative to keep the program going, and in 1961, a repletion initiative started. Through this expanded annual seed and shell program, "fossil" shell was dredged up from silted-over, non-productive oyster bars. Then it was washed and replanted on public oyster beds. Some shells were also distributed over 1,200 acres of protected seeding areas, in order to transfer the shell after spat-settlement to areas open for public harvest. Watermen were contracted to help in this effort, dredging shell and planting seeded oysters in locations that the state and the county oystermen committees identified together.

This arrangement was unarguably beneficial to the watermen. In the stable years of a regular harvest, it worked well and provided multiple opportunities along the way for oyster harvesters to find state work in otherwise slack seasons. For twenty years, it was the gold standard of large-scale oyster cultivation, and public bars flourished under the influx of dredged and washed shell and viable seed.

Paul Kellam, a commercial waterman from St. Mary's County, recalled the seed program fondly:

> Well, the state had a program, we used to have large spat sets in certain areas, and they'd put shells overboard, these fossil shells that they'd bring from up around Baltimore, and transplant them beside a productive oyster bar, and the spat from the oyster bar would catch on the shells, and they'd send the oystermen out to take the shells and transplant them in different parts of the Bay that were not necessarily good for catching spat, but better for growing.[100]

The seed program ushered in decades of salad days in the Chesapeake, according to Kellam and other watermen, not just because of the productive oyster business but also because so many aspects of the seasonal fishery cycle were intact:

> There's no comparison now to what it was when I started. I mean, the water business was 12 months a year then, and there was many a different fisheries you could get into. If oystering wasn't too good you could put out gill nets. And if gill netting wasn't any good, about the time of late winter, you'd go hauling seed, or dredging oysters, or you'd have crab pots in the summer, or trot lining. There's no opportunities now compared to then. Everybody's forced into one fishery, and that's through regulation.[101]

The growing demand for oyster shell, utilized as part of the state's oyster repletion program, reflected the transformed farming environment of the

Chesapeake Bay. Since World War II, chemical fertilizers and advances in modern farming have taken a dramatic toll on both the Bay's water quality and its oyster populations.

During the war, nitrogen was produced in enormous quantities at U.S. factories to meet the demand for explosives. In the postwar period, synthetic nitrogen was returned to its original use—as fertilizer. Remarkably versatile, industrially synthesized nitrogen was now touted as a way to feed the world. The industry transitioned easily from munitions to fertilizer, fueled by the proliferation of new strains of high-yield, fertilizer-dependent corn. Today, walls of emerald corn envelop highways along Maryland's Eastern Shore and Pennsylvania's arable Susquehanna watershed, all flourishing thanks to copious infusions of chemical fertilizers.

Synthetic nitrogen would eventually transform the traditional, diverse agricultural model of the United States to the modern monoculture that dominates farming today. Corn is at the center of that monoculture, representing 30 percent of the United States' agricultural production.[102] Applications of nitrogen and its brother nutrient, phosphorus, are incredibly effective ways for farmers to dramatically increase their yield. However, they are just as encouraging to algae growth as they are feed corn when they are not taken up by plants in the field. In the modern Bay, fertilizer-fed algae blooms grow toward the water's surface in summer, shading native grass beds on the bottom and causing oxygen-deprived "dead zones" when they invariably wilt and are consumed by bacteria. Though mobile organisms like fish and crabs can swim away from these dead zones, oysters are trapped and suffocate.

The flooding spring rains carry more than fertilizer to harm the Chesapeake's oysters. Old oyster beds are often covered by inches of silt—the black, fertile topsoil washed off the Chesapeake's millions of cultivated acres. Dredges have made oysters particularly susceptible to smothering by this thick, dense sediment. Working like collapsing machines, dredges break down the vertical structure of an oyster's reef and spread it along the bottom in two-dimensional bars. This makes it easier to scrape oysters up in the dredge's heavy teeth and in many cases can help individual oysters grow larger without competition, but accumulating sediment can quickly cover these flattened bars. Influxes of cleansed shell can help lift oysters off the bottom while encouraging fresh sets of spat on the sediment-free cultch, but as the sediment piles up, more and more shell is needed to provide new landing pads for free-floating spat.

The 1960s demand for clean shell was one of the first indications that the Chesapeake's growing sediment was an environmental problem with greater impacts than just muddy water. As once-sandy bottoms became pillowed by feet of silt from the region's farms, the areas of viable bottom for oyster bars shrank. Still-productive bars needed more shell to stay above the encroaching mud, which sifted down with every heavy rain.

The rapid postwar agricultural changes on land in the Chesapeake Bay were environmental time bombs. Band-Aid measures like shell repletion efforts would prop up declining oyster populations if conditions deteriorated slowly and gradually. Oysters smothered under layers of silt, and broadcasting spat were confronted by bottoms of uninhabitable mud instead of oyster reefs. The amount of suspended sediment and free-floating algae was more than even the massive oyster populations of the Jamestown era could have efficiently filtered.

The tenacious oysters that managed to survive in this degraded environment had more than mud to contend with. Between 1955 and 1965, Dermo and MSX infected Virginia's oyster beds, devastating the population and reducing the state's oyster harvest by half.[103] The shell and seed program, it would later turn out, had unwittingly helped the spread of the two diseases. As the state of Maryland arranged for oysters to be moved from productive southern Maryland rivers and seeded on northern beds, infected oysters hitched a free ride. Scientists hoped by relocating diseased oysters to the lower salinities of the upper Bay, the fresh water would inhibit the disease's transmission and allow the oysters to mature to legal size. It was a gamble for a short-term benefit that would prove to have long-term consequences.

Initially, the northern oyster beds benefited from the influx of spat. Between 1960 and 1967, Maryland's oyster harvest doubled, from 1.5 to 3 million bushels per year—the highest oyster yield in almost three decades and the first time that Maryland's production had ever eclipsed that of Virginia in the twentieth century. It was a period of optimism for the Chesapeake's watermen. Water work seemed like a stable occupation for the first time in several generations, and many young men applied for commercial fishing licenses. The new profusion of oysters was established on a shaky foundation, however. Sleeping among the thriving spat were dormant diseases, waiting to be revived when the Upper Bay's salinity inevitably increased.

As positive effects of the shell replenishment initiatives turned up in dredges and tongs, Maryland relaxed its regulations in 1967, allowing watermen to start harvesting oysters under power two days a week. Although outboard and in-board marine engines had existed for decades, Maryland had intentionally restricted watermen to harvesting under sail as a way to manage the fishery. In that same round of legislation, the state redoubled its efforts with the shell repletion program, earmarking state revenues for the program and increasing taxes on oystermen.[104] By increasing shell replenishment while easing restrictions, the state hoped to encourage a self-sustaining, non-subsidized oystering industry.

The oyster repletion efforts were considerably more expensive than estimated, however—hardly a surprise given the environmental difficulties plaguing the oyster population. In 1969, though payments into Maryland's fisheries fund totaled over $900,000, expenditures for resource management hit almost $1.5 million—a deficit that only continued to grow.[105] The beautiful, anachronistic skipjack fleet continued to leave harbors for uncertain harvests. Their engines now firing two days a week, they dredged for oysters that more often were planted by the state rather than a true wild population. Ironically, given the Maryland watermen's rejection of private oyster culture, this was indeed cultivation—just as statewide, public initiative, rather than individual, private one.

Trouble lay just on the horizon for Maryland's oyster industry, which had so far managed to survive in spite of the diseases ravaging Virginia's oysters. Buffered by fresh water and bolstered by shell and seed, the watermen's increasing harvests were tenuous. All it would take was one perfect storm for the Chesapeake's fragile ecological balancing act to dramatically—and some say irreversibly—change forever. It arrived in 1972, during one of the wettest springs in the Chesapeake that anyone could recall.

In early June, a storm developed to hurricane intensity north of Cuba. The Chesapeake watershed was already saturated after an unusually wet winter and spring in 1972, and farmers had been delayed plowing and fertilizing their fields. Rain had continued to fall through the first few weeks of June, and the latest storm on June 14 drenched the region with another three inches. The hurricane—named "Agnes"—arrived on June 21. Just as a thin veil of green corn and soybeans were sprouting on the region's many farms, Agnes came in with a torrent of endless water. In just three days, from June 21 through June 23, the Susquehanna and Potomac bloated with an excess of eight inches of rainfall each, swelling over the banks of the main rivers and barreling through the communities along the waterways.

In Elmira, New York, in a distant reach of the Chesapeake watershed, surprising debris raced on to the top of the floodwaters, headed to the Susquehanna. An eyewitness later recalled, "There are images that are ingrained in my mind from that time: the dead horse on the shoulder of the road by my aunt's house, the caskets that floated into people's front yards, the cars stuck up in the branches in a tree. The things I saw! Houses lifted clear off their foundations, a baby that was washed out of his mother's arms during their harrowing escape from the floodwater."[106]

The floodwaters would storm through the tangled rivers of the watershed, arriving at the Bay's main stem a few days later. Writer and historian Kent Mountford later recalled observing the dramatic before-and-after effects of the hurricane while on a sailing trip on June 24:

> *A fine afternoon at anchor, I took my waterproof camera and dove underwater to chase schools of silversides. Visibility was about 4 feet…we sailed out into the Chesapeake and found the Bay quite clear and the first cownose rays of the season appeared off Drum Point in midriver, which (was) not yet showing any silt from the hurricane. We ran back into the river for the night and entering the adjacent creeks found a veritable "wall" of sediment heading for the Bay, as sharp a boundary as if one poured cream into coffee—four foot visibility on one side, barely an inch of visibility in the mass of coming sediment. The effects of this would prove profound.*[107]

The topsoil and rainwater of three states exploded down the Susquehanna and into the placid, shallow body of the Chesapeake Bay. Thick with debris, it scoured the immense underwater meadows of the Susquehanna flats and continued south toward the open ocean. The fifty-three flood control gates of the Conowingo Dam at the base of the Susquehanna River were opened, spewing fourteen years' worth of trapped sediment—almost 50 million tons. Much of it was rich with chemical fertilizers, which settled thickly in drifts of mud up to twenty-five centimeters deep and fed summer algae blooms for years to come.

In the following days, when the floodwaters had receded, a new, unfamiliar Chesapeake emerged from the destruction. Ten acres of new Chesapeake islands were formed. Eelgrasses were ripped from the Bay's bottom almost completely—only 11 percent remained in sparse patches after Agnes came through. The blasting water had also banished shad and herring eggs and larvae from the freshwater nurseries on Bay tributaries—estimates later gauged that as many as 6.5 million per hour had been ejected from the Rappahannock River alone.[108]

The freshwater from Agnes completely unbalanced the delicate salinity of the northern Chesapeake. Oysters north of the Chesapeake Bay Bridge suffered 100 percent mortalities, and watermen from Rock Hall or Havre de Grace pulled up the gaping casualties when they experimentally lowered their dredges in the fall. The oysters in the Potomac, a traditionally rich harvesting area, also died. Agnes would cast a shadow over the oyster populations for years to come. In 1972 and '73, the Bay's low salinity and dense sediment were so persistent they stopped oyster reproduction not once but twice. A waterman from Cobb's Island in southern Maryland later recalled, "You could see the oysters that had rotted in the shells and floated to the top of the river, on top of the water. We went back later on and checked it, it was nothing but shells. Every oyster had died from the Potomac River and Wicomico River. I guess we lost millions of bushels of oysters."[109]

Before Agnes, it had been twenty years since any truly devastating storms had impacted the Chesapeake. After 1972, however, a series of catastrophic tropical storms and hurricanes blew through the Chesapeake regularly: Eloise in 1975; David in 1979; Gloria in 1985; Fran in 1996, Floyd in 1999; Isabel in 2003; Frances, Ivan and Jeanne in 2004; and Tropical Storm Lee and Hurricane Irene in 2011. Although none came as early in the season as Agnes—truly the perfect storm—each event brought more freshwater, more sediment and more nutrients flooding into the Chesapeake, settling on top of bottom murky from the last major storm. Perhaps without the consequences of human habitation, the Chesapeake Bay watershed might have rebounded from these meteorological onslaughts. Instead, the streak of sediment the stormwater carries down the Bay's main stem, observable from space, serves as an ugly, regular reminder of the pressures our farming, our development and our effluent have created.

The unprecedented ravages of Hurricane Agnes were impossible to ignore, especially in a Chesapeake Bay community that was becoming more aware of the dramatic changes in the environment. In 1967, the Chesapeake Bay Foundation was established with the mission of Chesapeake Bay advocacy and research. Its motto, "Save the Bay," conveyed the sense of foreboding felt by the Bay's first generation of environmentalists. Across the United States, millions could relate. Industry and growth were unchecked, and their impact on the water, air and the land had been accumulating for almost one hundred years. The Cuyahoga River, full of industrial effluent, caught on fire in 1969. Authors like Rachel Carson decried the spoiled landscape and the detriment to living creatures in her 1962 book *Silent Spring*, which laid out her environmental rallying cry: "Our heedless and destructive acts enter into the vast cycles of the earth and in time return to bring hazard to ourselves."

By the inaugural Earth Day rally in 1970, national environmental consciousness had officially awoken. This sweeping change in public perception directly impacted the Chesapeake. The Clean Water Act was passed in 1972, regulating wastewater discharge and dredged material and encouraging conservation practices. In 1973, the Army Corps of Engineers issued an alarming study stating that between 1940 and 1970, the Bay's population had doubled.

The study reported that unlike the Cuyahoga's industrial pollution, the Chesapeake's problems were a direct result of ever more people living, working and playing in the watershed.[110] The Chesapeake Bay, it seemed, suffered from a paradox. It was the very beauty of the Bay's open rivers and verdant marshes that were responsible for encouraging staggering population growth and all its negative effects in the watershed. A study of the Chesapeake Bay by the Environmental Protection Agency in 1976 echoed this finding. "Up until the EPA studies," said Fran Flanigan, executive director of the Alliance for the Chesapeake, "people always blamed 'Mother Nature.' 'It was a big system.' 'Things moved in cycles.' After the EPA study, we realized that there were human impacts."[111]

In the aftermath of Hurricane Agnes and its devastating effects on the Chesapeake oyster populations, the Chesapeake Biological Laboratory at the University of Maryland Center for Environmental Science (UMCES) set about testing the potential for rehabilitating the wasted stocks. Hired right out of St. Mary's College to work on the study was a young biologist from the heart of Chesapeake oyster country, Don "Mutt" Meritt. Meritt had already spent years working with oysters as a waterman out of St. Michaels. He tonged for oysters in the winter and trotlined in the summer all through college and said of his upbringing, "It was pretty natural to know what was going on in the water. All you needed was a license and a boat and you could go do it. You were your own boss."[112]

As with William K. Brooks's earlier work with the Chesapeake Zoological Laboratory in 1879, Meritt found himself almost one hundred years later working for the same goal: to restore oyster populations in order to sustain the oyster economy. In his first few years with UMCES, the university moved the lab to the Eastern Shore of Maryland, on an isolated neck on LeCompte Bay known as Horn Point. There, Meritt set about producing oyster larvae—a lot of them. Horn Point labs first produced a "modest" 1 million oyster larvae, and over the years, production has grown to a staggering 75 million per year.

As Meritt busily coaxed oysters to reproduce at Horn Point Labs—a process the straight-talking scientist has referred to as "oyster porn"—the Chesapeake environment continued to decline, weathering frequent storms, increased turbidity and, in the 1980s, the recurring devastation of MSX and Dermo on the Bay's oyster populations. His hatchery, initially designed to

A new batch of oyster spat at Horn Point Laboratory. *Photo by Jay Fleming.*

produce oysters for commercial harvest, has now become Maryland's most important producer of seed for oyster reserves and sanctuaries.

The catalyst for this sea change can be traced back to a single paper. Written by another UMCES staffer, Roger Newell, in 1988, the paper made a groundbreaking claim: oyster population decline and the environmental tailspin of the Chesapeake Bay were connected. Newell's research, responding to the increase in the size and frequency of the Bay's summer dead zones throughout the 1980s, proposed that the "pre-1870 oyster populations in the Chesapeake Bay could potentially filter the entire water column during the summer in less than 3 to 6 days." Between disease and the combined onslaught of sediment and nutrients, that natural filtration of the Chesapeake had slowed to a crawl, with the process now taking almost a year. The solution was easy, Newell suggested. Simply, "an increase in the oyster population by management and aquaculture could significantly improve water quality."[113]

Oysters as panacea for the Chesapeake's manifold ills was a mightily appealing concept. According to Newell's study, as an all-natural, all-native solution to the Bay's suspended sediment and algae, oysters couldn't be beat. Newell's later work even showed oyster reefs to be handy digesters of nitrogen, too—encouraging the growth of good bacteria that tackled the nutrients remaining after a trip through an oyster's digestive system.[114]

It was timely news. The Chesapeake's oxygen deserts, sustained by nutrient-fed algae, were occurring more frequently. Throughout the 1980s, more than 40 percent of the Bay experienced "air droughts" in the summertime when the oxygen in the water dipped below the amount required to sustain life. These events, called "crab jubilees" by old-timers, were a sign of a deep imbalance in the Bay's environment. They were also unsettling to behold. Kent Mountford, the same man who had witnessed Agnes's arrival in the Chesapeake a few years earlier, described a 1981 crab jubilee for the *Bay Journal*:

> *"As we descended a steep road to the Bay, the water looked different: It was bright Caribbean blue. People were wading in the shallows with crab nets. Some had bushel baskets jammed in the doughnut hole of an automobile inner tube.*
>
> *In the shallows, submerged in only a few inches of water, crabs were stacked up in rows as dense as cars in a parking lot. There were a lot of other species: small fish and flounder struggling along at the edge where tiny waves lapped the shore, their upper gill covers literally rising into the air in a desperate search for oxygen. To this day, the memory of it still strikes me as remarkably sad.*[115]

If the Chesapeake Bay could be saved from a future of crab jubilees, it was clear that the restoration of a healthy and thriving oyster population should be a top priority. But after several years of drought intensified the Upper Bay's salinity, the Bay's oyster populations were in the throes of MSX and Dermo's blight. The oysters that had been moved from disease-stricken shoals on the lower Bay to beds on the Upper Bay with the hopes that low salinity would prevent the spread of the two parasites were now inevitably riddled with MSX and Dermo. More than ever, science needed to identify a way to make more (hopefully disease-resistant) oysters—for the watermen and for the environment. Mutt Meritt and his team fell to the task at Horn Point Laboratories, while at the Virginia Institute of Marine Science, an oyster biologist, Stan Allen, did the same with his lab.

All stakeholders anxiously waited, while the headlines grew grimmer. "Praying for Rain in the Bay: Oystermen Hope Something Can Wash Away the Parasites," declared the *Washington Post* in 1995. Maryland watermen gamely left their harbors to harvest what oysters might have survived, but there was nothing there to catch. That year, Virginia's harvest was at a miniscule 7,401 bushels, while Maryland's was at a still-paltry 160,000 bushels—a number that had been only reached by redoubling the costly seed repletion efforts, underwritten by a one-dollar-per-bushel harvest tax.[116]

In 1993, watermen, scientists, environmentalists and other stakeholders sat down to talk about the Chesapeake's oyster problems and what could be done to address it. The "Oyster Roundtable," convened by the State of Maryland, aimed to find collaborative solutions or, at the very least, to open a dialogue on disease, water quality, production and funding for restoration initiatives. Amazingly, all actions endorsed by the group had to be unanimous—a staggering feat, given the conflicting politics and goals represented by the group's members. The fact that only eighty thousand bushels had been harvested that year proved to be a strong motivator, however.[117] Working together, the group was able to reach a consensus and published a list of recommendations in December 1993.

Many of the goals proposed by the Oyster Roundtable were common-sense restrictions on questionable practices—stopping the spread of diseased oysters around the state's tributaries through the seed program, for example. Other recommendations took common sense a step further. The Roundtable endorsed an aquaculture program complete with permits and support from Maryland's Department of Natural Resources—a radical departure for Maryland's traditionally privatization-averse commercial fishery. It also recommended the establishments of Oysters Recovery Areas (ORAs). ORAs as the Roundtable conceived them were essentially sanctuaries with differing levels of harvest allowances. These sanctuaries would be living laboratories—protected oyster bars where experimentation with reef structure, density and, hopefully, disease resistance could take place. The ORAs would also provide a baseline understanding of how oysters provided habitat for spat and other Bay species.

To oversee their recommendations, including sanctuaries and an overhauled seed program, the Oyster Roundtable called for the establishment of a nonprofit facilitator, a body it named the "Oyster Recovery Partnership." It was a groundbreaking concept and, with its primary focus of promoting the ecological restoration of oysters in the Chesapeake Bay, a commendable one.

However, it was difficult to take the idea for the Oyster Recovery Partnership off the paper and into reality. In theory, the nonprofit would operate on private funds, but in practice, the group struggled with inadequate financial and staff support. By 2000, when Charles Frentz was hired as executive director, the partnership only got $450,000 from NOAA.[118] The grand sanctuaries-cum-laboratories in the Oyster Roundtable's vision were in fact miniscule plots of planted oysters, seeded by volunteers. Fortunately, Frentz was a savvy networker and encouraged Mutt Meritt at Horn Point hatchery to ramp up production of seed oysters while also persuading Senator Barbara Mikulski to increase earmark funding for the partnership.

Frentz saw the problems in the state's continuation of its seed program, which still proceeded as usual even though it continued to spread diseased oysters around the Bay. Instead, he proposed watermen use Oyster Recovery Partnership's disease-resistant seed, sourced from Horn Point lab. These would be available for harvest on special "managed reserves," with one catch—watermen would have to wait until the oysters were four inches in size—one inch larger than the state normally required. This turned out to be a fatal flaw in Frentz's plan. During an argument with a waterman who was irate over the added inch restriction, Larry Simns—head of the Maryland Watermen's Association and Oyster Recovery Partnership board member—had a culling hammer thrown at his head.[119] The ORP compromised, changing the restriction to state that once half the bar's oysters reached four inches, watermen could also harvest the three-inch oysters, too.

The goals of the Oyster Recovery Partnership were true to the Oyster Roundtable that had created it—to improve the environment and sustain the fishery. While the ORP created sanctuaries, it also planted oysters on managed reserves for eventual harvest and on public bars for unrestricted harvesting. One hundred or even sixty years ago, these efforts would have been lauded. But in the twenty-first-century Chesapeake, where the low oyster populations were often blamed on watermen's overharvesting, the ORP's efforts were often criticized as little more than subsidies to support watermen.

Public backlash particularly focused on ORP's bar-cleaning program, which hired contracted watermen to remove diseased oysters from a bar before it was seeded with Horn Point oysters. Watermen were happy to do the work, which took place in the spring—usually a slack season. The diseased oysters they harvested were often set aside for later harvest and commercial sale—a process that ensured watermen were paid twice, for bar-cleaning and then for selling the ORP's unwanted oysters. Simns managed the program, a paid ORP position, for which he also came under fire. But at the end of the day, many saw the ORP's efforts as the only thing stopping Maryland's oystermen from disappearing forever as disease crippled the industry. "Everyone who participates likes it, for the income if nothing else," said Bunky Chance, a Talbot County waterman, of the bar-cleaning program. "Most watermen are just trying to keep the wolf from the door."[120]

By 2006, the Chesapeake had sixty oyster sanctuaries, with half of those in the Maryland portion of the Chesapeake Bay. The Oyster Recovery Partnership continued to contribute to the sanctuaries but also continued its work with the managed reserves—a program that grew in importance when the State of Maryland largely discontinued its own wild seed program in 2004. ORP also made strides in sourcing shell for restoration, convincing restaurants to join a "Shell Recycling Alliance" rather than dumping useful clutch into the trash.

In 2008, ORP joined the Maryland Department of Natural Resources and the Horn Point Lab hatchery on a new initiative—oyster gardening. In this public awareness program, hundreds of Chesapeake waterfront property owners agreed to suspend immature oysters in cages from their docks, with the goal of planting them on local sanctuaries. These efforts expanded on some of the experimentation by early oyster gardening activists like Len Zuza and Jim McVey and organizations like the Chesapeake Bay Foundation.[121] The goal of oyster gardening was Bay restoration, rather than oyster fishery restoration, with the thought that seeing the biodiversity and water quality impacts of oysters firsthand would help create new Chesapeake stewards.

The program succeeded in introducing thousands of people to the incredible habitat and sheer filtering ability of an oyster reef. It also underscored the divided world of Chesapeake oysters. Prior to the impacts of MSX and Dermo, oyster restoration was solely focused on producing more oysters for the fishery. After MSX and Dermo, and with the surge of interest in Chesapeake environmentalism, oyster restoration also focused on oysters as the keystone of an overall Bay improvement plan.

These two goals—more oysters for the watermen and more oysters for environmental restoration—though seemingly complementary, were frequently at odds. Indeed, oyster environmentalists and oyster harvesters were regularly pitted against one another in the media, online, in political arenas and in public discourse. Watermen were criticized for continuing to harvest even as disease ravaged the oyster population and for participating in what many saw as a state-subsidized "put and take" fishery. Their harvesting methods also came under scrutiny, especially power dredging, which the State of Maryland opened into three counties in 1999 and later expanded in 2003 as a way to aid struggling watermen.

Power dredging allowed motorized workboats to harvest oysters by dredge. This was a major departure from the traditional skipjack regulations, which allowed dredging by pushboat only two days a week, with dredging under sail required the rest of the time. Power dredging was very efficient, and watermen felt that it had the added benefit of picking oysters and cultch out of the mud in a process they referred to as "fluffing the bottom." Whether it benefited the oyster bottom or not, it was an effective way of sustaining the beleaguered oyster harvest—by 2005, power-dredged oysters represented 79 percent of the twenty-six thousand overall bushels harvested in Maryland.[122]

Modern waterman power dredging. *Photo by Jay Fleming.*

While popular among watermen, critics decried power dredging as a clear example of overharvesting. Environmental groups—which envisioned a restored, clear Chesapeake with soaring oyster reefs—particularly disliked how dredges broke down vertical oyster structures. In their view, power dredging created a two-dimensional, easily worked bar—a practice environmentalists felt had no ecological benefit if it left oysters flat on the oxygen-starved Bay bottom to be buried by silt.

Watermen, on the other hand, criticized the remove of environmentalists from the day-to-day realities of oystering. From their perspective, scientific practices developed in a laboratory setting did not always suit the real-world environment of the Chesapeake's oyster bars, which they observed firsthand. The increase in taxes and regulations, informed by conservation practices, were at odds with the watermen's needs to earn a living as efficiently as possible. Alternative solutions to oyster decline, like sanctuaries or aquaculture, were often dismissed as unworkable or purposefully onerous.

As the state of Maryland considered the question of an Asian oyster introduction and later, sanctuaries, the opposing views of the oyster stakeholders were starkly illuminated at public forums. "I'd just like to say that I can't see how the sanctuaries are going to work when the shells they want to reclaim get silted over and they want to restrict power dredging more and more,"[123] commented a Rock Hall waterman at a public hearing on July 7, 2010. At the same hearing, a representative from the Chesapeake Bay Foundation countered, "I'd like to remind everyone that these oyster are, in fact, a public resource and owned by every citizen of Maryland. I believe that setting aside 25 percent of that publicly-owned resource in order to help improve the water quality in the Bay, and to help ensure a long-term sustainability of our oyster population is scientifically sound and long overdue."[124]

The expanded sanctuaries proposed by Maryland's governor in 2009 accompanied the sweeping state stance on aquaculture and left many of Maryland's traditional oyster harvesters feeling left in the lurch. Dorchester County waterman "Boo" Powley summed up the collective helpless feelings of many watermen on the initiative:

> *This is a government take over. The government's got the banks. The government's got the car industry. Now, they got the health care. They're going to take everything in our lives. Now, they're coming for a bottom that's been public. It won't be public no more. You'll be lucky to even take your hook and line and go fishing on it. That's a shame. We're losing freedom so fast it makes me sick. They're going to listen to special interest groups to*

*pay lobbyists over here in Annapolis and you all need to pay attention to the stuff that's working down in Dorchester and Somerset County. We got oysters down there like you wouldn't believe and it didn't cost the taxpayers a dime.*[125]

The aggressive shift to embrace aquaculture and sanctuaries while limiting the public oyster harvest marked a sea change for Maryland's oystering watermen. One hundred years earlier, their political clout was unparalled, and their interests guided legislative efforts in Annapolis. However, with Maryland's Democratic governor Martin O'Malley's progressive environmental agenda, the watermen's fortunes had changed. Rather than continuing to invest in oysters for a public fishery, O'Malley directed state funding for initiatives to help watermen transition to aquaculture.

Some of Maryland's traditionally most productive bottom, tributaries that in prior years had been crowded with oysters, were turned into sanctuaries where public harvesting was permanently closed. "We can do better—we need to do better," O'Malley intoned as he unrolled his Chesapeake plan in Annapolis in December 2009. "Our economy needs this shot in the arm; our watermen need this shot in the arm. Certainly these waters have supported a lot of families for a lot of years, and we want to make sure that we do what we must in our own bay so that the bay can support jobs and livelihoods for years to come."[126]

The Maryland director of the Chesapeake Bay Foundation praised O'Malley, enthusing, "The state is finally and truly recognizing the ecological value of oysters." The 250-member Maryland's Oystermen Association decidedly disagreed. "It's a sad day," commented the executive director Jim Mullin. "They're going to take a culture and heritage and push it under the rug."[127] Despite the division in public sentiment, the push for aquaculture and sanctuaries as O'Malley's solution to the oyster problem moved forward. Both parts of the initiative would meet resistance along the way, but none were more visible or more dramatic than the standoff on the Little Choptank.

The sanctuaries, especially those proposed in Harris Creek and the Little Choptank River, were substantial in size and ultimately encompassed 24 percent of Maryland's viable oyster bars. By closing major stretches of rivers and entire still-productive tributaries, the state hoped to create large-scale oyster habitat restored with millions of dollars worth of cultch and Horn Point spat. These improved sanctuaries would, in theory, be spat factories, flooding the surrounding rivers with freshets of viable new oysters every summer. They would also allow the state to gauge the real possibility that the wild oyster populations could be developing resistance to MSX and Dermo.

The problem for watermen lay in the addition of cultch to these expansive new sanctuaries. Although off-limits to oystering, they were still open to other harvests. Crabbing, in particular, had grown in importance as oystering slowly waned. The best bottom for crabbing was grassy and flat, allowing watermen to place their crab pots and trotlines without fouling. The best bottom for growing oysters, scientists discerned, was the opposite—raised, irregular reef structures that provided plenty of nooks for drifting oyster larvae to latch. To create these artificial reefs, the state began to lay substrate. Mounds of concrete or fossilized shell were placed, sometimes up to two feet in height, on sanctuary bottoms and encrusted with millions of spat on shell. The sanctuary projects were so extensive, however, that Maryland quickly had to look beyond the Chesapeake for sources of the shell that were the preferred bottom material.

It was the Florida shell that angered the watermen. In 2014 alone, Maryland ordered 112,500 tons for sanctuaries—enough to cover eighty football fields to a depth of one foot.[128]

The Florida substrate was laced with fine sediments. Though representatives from Maryland's Department of Natural Resources assured the public the material was fine for substrate use, the local watermen predicted the chalky silt would ruin the sanctuary bottom for crabbing. "The stuff that's in that barge is not shells, I don't know what it is," remarked Scott Todd, president of the Dorchester Seafood Harvesters Association. "It's just mostly sludge and mud and it's nothing that anything is going to stick to and get a spat set on." The solution the watermen proposed—power dredging, the last thing reef restorationists would want—indicated the polarity of the issue's sides: "There are shells there, we saw them on our depth sounders here, we can see the shells that are ten or twelve inches under. There are plenty of shells there, we didn't have to go to Florida to buy shells."[129]

The Florida shell, silty or not, was headed to the Little Choptank to be spread over 187 acres of clear bottom. Already unharvestable for oysters due to sanctuary restrictions, the watermen feared they would now lose the Little Choptank crab harvest, too, as it was smothered under a foot of oyster shells and sediment. But there were future hopes for the sanctuary's oysters, too, that caused consternation. According to Scott Todd, the Little Choptank was "the most productive spot on Earth for oystering," adding, "They are permanently going to damage it. We're going to definitely do the best we can to stop this."

On May 1, 2014, they made good on their promise. As the sun rose over the calm Little Choptank, eleven workboats confronted the barges piled high with Florida shell. Surrounding the barge, engines idling in a fine rain, they settled in. Five hours later, the state called it. Work would not proceed for the day. It was a triumph for the watermen but a short-lived one. Work continued as usual the next day, with a large crane filling its bucket with Florida shell and dumping it into the shallow water of the Little Choptank, a river that had just been the site of the last and latest conflict of a modern-day Oyster War.

In this new era of the Chesapeake Bay, with aquaculture ascendant, young watermen have to get creative. While some protest aquaculture lease applications or lobby for change through watermen's associations in Annapolis, some have quietly started experimenting. The State of Maryland's aquaculture lease applicants, in fact, are largely watermen, looking to add another harvesting technique to their season-spanning repertoire.

Mark Connolly from Talbot County is one of these watermen. Now, he doesn't mind sharing that he has some issues with aquaculture—that oysters grown in farms can be sold, even in summer; that water-column leases can negatively impact clamming and other harvests—but he's applied for a lease in an area where he learned to hand-tong that is a sanctuary today. Leasing is allowed in sanctuaries, and his application is for a tributary of Harris Creek. He explained, "It only makes sense to go out and get a couple acres. I would do bottom aquaculture first. Go buy your seed, and get some shells, do the things they want you to do, and see if it works. If it costs you $3,000 or $4,000, that's money well spent in trying *something*. If it works, it works, and if it doesn't, we're out a couple thousand. Start out small, grow with it, and see how it fits your life."

For Connolly, the jury is still out on sanctuaries, however. He would have rather have seen a closed tributary or even an oyster license buy-back program before he saw a restoration project.

"Some of the things they think of are so out there. Oysters were coming back in Harris Creek. All they had to do was shut it down. That creek is not meant to have stones or rubble or stuff from Florida. You're messing with the environment. And once you put that stuff there, and you realize, maybe you've messed up, who is going to get it out of there?" Connolly takes a breath and then continues, "They poo-hooed and puffed around with that Asian oyster enough, it didn't seem like it took them no time, bang, bang, bang—sanctuary. Done. Bring the stones. If Mother Nature wanted stones, she'd have put them there. They call it habitat, I call it a mess."

For now, sanctuaries and aquaculture are here to stay throughout the Chesapeake. It is still, as Connolly points out, a period of experimentation.

The restoration of wild oyster populations is an unprecedented process. Everywhere else the native oyster stocks have dwindled, aquaculture took over without a backward glance at the happy days when shoals reached the shoreline. The Chesapeake, treating its oysters as part of an environmental remedy as well as an economic staple, has no example to follow. Guidebooks on how to rebuild an oyster population simply don't exist. And as Mutt Meritt, straight-talking Horn Point Lab scientist points out, what are we restoring the Bay's oysters to? "Bringing them back to what? To what they were when John Smith sailed up the Bay? To 1980, to 1990, to 1950? All over the state of Maryland? All over the Chesapeake Bay? There's all sorts of caveats to that. Everybody you talk to wants the bay to be back to what it was in 1960," Meritt says. "I'd like to have the body I had back in 1960—ain't gonna happen."[130]

CHAPTER 8

# THE CULTIVATED CHESAPEAKE

The drive to the Choptank Oyster Company sloughs away the years like onionskin. The road through Cambridge passes nineteenth-century shotgun houses of cannery workers from its oyster heyday, when the harbor was crowded with busy packinghouses. Each one is exactly the same as its neighbor except for its own distinctive decay: a sagging porch, curled roof shingles, a jungle of a yard with a lone lilac bush in bloom. There hasn't been oyster money in this town for quite a long time.

The houses give way to farmland, flat and wide. Turn right at the latticed arm of the Spocott windmill and head down a dirt road that parts the loblollies with a barber-like tidiness. The road eventually concludes at a ramshackle manor house. Unexpectedly, far to the right, a pile of oyster shells and shambling stacks of white PVC frames can only mean one thing—an oyster farm. A few pickup trucks are pulled over, beds mounded with the rugged orange plastic baskets of the watermen's trade. The real activity is focused around one long finger of dock that extends into the Choptank. Surrounded by a halo of white, floating frames, workers sort and pack the oysters into white cardboard boxes for the half-shell market. A big plywood table on sawhorses is mounded up with oysters, the smell of them briny, metallic, richly organic.

The guy in charge is Kevin McClarren. He is usually kitted out in layers of fleeces and a big pair of mud-splattered waders, and he oversees a few

Cambridge, Maryland's bustling waterfront was a hub of the Bay's oystering industry in the early twentieth century. Today, all but one of the once-numerous seafood packing businesses are gone. *Chesapeake Bay Maritime Museum Collections.*

guys in the water turning cages or rummaging through the piled-up oysters to prepare shipments for the day. He starts his day at sunrise, and if he hasn't knocked off at three for a cold brew after long hours toiling in the Choptank, he counts the day at a loss. He's opinionated about oysters and plenty of other things, but his iconoclastic streak works for him. After all, you have to be something of a strong-willed individual to manage one of the first oyster farms in Maryland, a state that's not known for rolling out the welcome mat for aquaculture.

When husband-and-wife team Bob Maze and Laurie Landau started the Choptank Oyster Company in 2004, there were only a handful of other oyster growers in the state. The largest was a public enterprise—Horn Point Laboratory, part of the University of Maryland's Center for Environmental Science, just across LeCompte Bay on the Choptank. Horn Point's spat were primarily going toward producing infant oysters for use in sanctuary restoration at the time. Unlike Virginia, which had an established aquaculture

Oyster farmer Kevin McClarren and his oyster floats at the Choptank Oyster Company. *Photo by author.*

industry as a result of its leasing-friendly historic fishery management policies, Maryland's approach had given lip service to bottom leasing but largely focused on a traditional harvest.

Initially, Marinetics (as it was named at the time) was a one-stop oyster shop. It used brood stock oysters to produce its own larvae and spat set and grew its oysters to maturity in its own floats along the shoreline of Castle Haven point. The business was so early on the forefront of Maryland oyster farming that cages on the bottom, the typical growing gear used today, weren't legal yet within the state (and wouldn't be until 2009). Since then, the business has streamlined. The overhauled chicken houses that used to grow spat sit empty since the Choptank Oyster Company took to purchasing its seed oysters from Horn Point Labs and other hatcheries. The change seems a fruitful one—along the docks, long white streamers of connected oyster floats trail off, testament to Maryland aquaculture's emerging era of salad days.

Today, the Choptank Oyster Company's annual sales are nearing the $1 million mark, and well-heeled foodies can purchase a dozen fresh, plump Choptank Sweets at Whole Foods. But these successes would have seemed improbable even fifteen years ago. Maryland has long been a state where working the water is a regional birthright, and generation after generation hands down the boats, tools and fishery traditions of the northern Chesapeake with little deviation. Aquaculture, with its reliance on costly technology and precise scientific methods, as well as its physical restriction to one patch of shoreline or bottom, is a sharp deviation from the peeling paint, heavy iron tools and wide-open freedom of a traditional oyster harvest.

Change comes slowly here, especially on the Eastern Shore, removed as it is from the traffic and suburbia of the Baltimore/Washington corridor. Here in the Land of Pleasant Living, oysters have always been wild, have always been cheap and have always been harvested by hardworking cowboys who rustle up their catch from the pillowy sediment of the Bay's bottom. Aquaculture is seen by many as a departure from that—as a challenge to time-honored traditions cherished by Marylanders.

The debate over aquaculture has become a Chesapeake tradition. Over a century ago, oyster leasing was introduced to the Chesapeake when the Bay's oyster economy was still thriving. The response from the Bay's nineteenth-century watermen was at best dubious and at worst acrimonious. Decades of red tape, lobbying and rowdy protests followed. Since then, a deep skepticism over aquaculture has become enshrined, and the same debates, chewing repeatedly over old issues, have echoed down the generations of Maryland watermen.

The long historical odds hindering oyster farming have meant that the few intrepid Maryland entrepreneurs, like the Choptank Oyster Company, have set out to cover territory unexplored for one hundred years. Through trial, error and doggedness, they have answered the questions posited decades ago for themselves. In return, they have found frustration in regulatory labyrinths, have lost a few thousand oysters through failed experimentation and, sometimes, have eventually turned a profit. They come from vastly different walks of life and experience—from finance guys to good old boys, retired watermen to English majors.

Although the roads that lead them to oyster aquaculture started at distant points, today they come together at a humming crossroads where the oyster economy, the Chesapeake environment, the locavore movement and local heritage intersect. The winds of change blow steadily across the Bay, and these oyster farmers have raised their sails to harness it. But it took quite a journey to travel this far. Aquaculture represents a sea change of enormous importance—and it took a collapse of the oyster population so precipitous as to be past all hope to even be considered. Two oyster diseases—MSX and Dermo—would change the Chesapeake's environment forever in the wake of their blight.

The first dead oysters showed up in the Gulf of Mexico in the 1940s. Initially, it was believed that the culprit was a fungus called *Dermocystidium marinum*, or "Dermo"—at least, that's what it was still called when it was first spread to the Chesapeake Bay in 1949. Upon further research, it turned out that the oysters were dying of a virulent little parasite ultimately named *Perkinsis marinus*, but the nickname "Dermo" stuck.[131]

Spread in high-salinity waters through the consumption of infected dead oyster detritus by healthy oysters during the warm months of May through July, Dermo is a nastily prodigious hitchhiker. As the infected oyster's growth, reproduction and overall health plummet, hundreds of thousands of parasites are swarming inside the oyster's system, ultimately taking over its oyster host. When the host inevitably disintegrates, the parasites then depart, off to new, unsullied specimens.

MSX, or *Haplosporidium nelsoni*, is a greater mystery than its earlier forerunner, Dermo. Its common name, MSX, even means "multinucleated sphere unknown." Although scientists are unsure how the disease is transmitted, its capacity for devastation has been clear. MSX was most likely introduced to the East Coast of the United States after World War II by the Asian oyster *Crassostrea gigas*, possibly in aquaculture use.[132]

In 1957, the parasite crippled the Delaware Bay's oyster populations, generating massive oyster mortalities. Just two years later, MSX was discovered in the lower Chesapeake Bay. Like Dermo, MSX is particular about season and salinity—found in water with salinity level at fifteen parts per thousand or above, the parasite affects the gills and mantle of infected oysters between mid-May through October.

Virginia, traditionally the larger oyster producer in the Chesapeake, was the first to feel the swift and ruinous impact of MSX and Dermo. Between 1955 and 1965, the National Marine Fish and Wildlife Service officially tallied Virginia's harvest (in pounds, not bushels) from over 21 millions pounds harvested per year to just over 12 million pounds harvested.[133] But the real devastation was yet to come. Although initially both MSX and Dermo were limited to the saltier waters of Virginia, a series of warm winters and summer drought conditions in the 1980s made much of the Chesapeake's main stem the optimal temperature and salinity for the spread of both diseases.

# CHESAPEAKE OYSTERS

The collapse was dramatic—Virginia's catch went from approximately 7.5 million pounds in 1980 to 1.5 million pounds in 1990, while Maryland's catch went from about 14 million pounds to fewer than 3 million in the same period. The early 1990s saw even steeper declines, with some slight recovery at the end of the decade after a few freshets of spring rains diluted the deadly salinity creeping up the Bay. By 2003, those gains had been lost and the harvest hit rock bottom: Maryland watermen had harvested 158,000 pounds, with the value of the total harvest worth only $706,000, and in Virginia, the 77,000 bushels harvested only brought in $263,000.[134]

For the watermen, the impact was crippling. Ed Farley, captain of the skipjack *HM Krentz*, commented on the enormous impact made by the oyster mortality on his business and way of life: "I'm just scared to death. I'm facing having to sell my boat and my house. If I don't have enough cash flow from oystering in the next few months, I don't know how I can survive."[135]

Some watermen like Farley moved toward the burgeoning heritage tourism market, an enterprise rising from the hogged, forgotten workboats and rusted tools abandoned by the flagging oyster business. Other watermen transitioned from a largely winter harvest to a summer one, focusing on fishing for the blue crab that was quickly taking the oyster's place as the defining seafood of the Chesapeake region.

In Virginia, where oyster leases had provided a healthy portion of the annual oyster harvest, watermen had to turn to other fisheries to survive. For many, hard clams provided a convenient alternative to the years of disappointment and financial risk posed by MSX and Dermo. Though wild hard or "cherrystone" clams had traditionally made up a piece of Virginia's seasonal harvests, it had never been more than a sideline supplement for regional watermen. But in the 1990s, that all began to change.

The Virginia Institute of Marine Science (VIMS) had developed aquaculture techniques for hard clams as far back as the 1960s, and Virginia watermen's bottom leases, now clotted with dead oyster "boxes" and useless cultch, were the perfect canvases for clam cultivation. At the H.M. Terry Company, where oysters had been produced since 1903 by three generations of the Terry family under the "Sewansecott" brand, clams proved to be a godsend. Working with the scientists at VIMS and through years of trial and error, Pete and Wec Terry were able to develop innovative methods of farming hard clams that helped the family business weather the hard times facing the oyster industry. They weren't alone. Between 1991 and 2004, Virginia's farmed hard clams grew from around 30 million sold to around 150 million sold—a 400 percent increase.[136]

Throughout Virginia's famed oyster bottom, bivalves were once again thriving—they just weren't oysters.

For many in Maryland, where the salinity was too low for clam farms and traditions favored wild harvests, the destruction of the oyster fishery represented the end of the line for work on the water. "Fish come and go," said president of the Maryland Waterman's Association Larry Simns in 2009. "You can't count on them, but the oysters and clams was the backbone of the watermen." Without the security of oysters, many watermen had to find work on land, getting along as best as they could without the guiding compass of their longstanding traditions. "They cut grass in the summer," Simns continued, "they work in marinas. A lot of them own tugboats…and in Smith Island and Crisfield a lot of people are working in the prison down there in Somerset County. It's not what they want to do; it's what they have to do."[137]

The Chesapeake's oyster population was in dire straits and the fishery along with it. A radical solution was needed. Although the traditions of the Chesapeake did not gladly welcome outside influence, the time was ripe for some hard-earned wisdom and scientific suggestions from decidedly non-Bay sources. Beyond the Chesapeake and its imperiled oyster fishery, there were working examples to follow—places in the United States and abroad that had suffered the collapse and eventual restoration of their regional oyster harvests.

In New England, the Pacific Northwest and as far as Britain and France, shellfish industries were once again flourishing—but the new iterations often looked radically different from the old wild fisheries that they replaced. Where native oyster populations had been almost completely fished out, oyster farms, some with stunningly advanced techniques, had taken their place. These were not luck-of-the-draw endeavors like wild oyster harvesting. Rather, these farms were assiduously tended by owner/cultivators who managed each stage of their oyster crop's development. Where native oyster stocks were decimated by disease, nonnative species were introduced that were untroubled by the parasites and viruses suffered by local varieties.

One hardy Asian species in particular, *Crassostrea gigas*, from Japan, was universally popular as a native replacement. Introduced around the world to bolster failing native populations, by 2003 it represented almost 99 percent of the international oyster harvest.[138]

In France, where the native *Crassostrea edulis* had been decimated by disease, *Crassostrea gigas* had been introduced by the ton to sanctuaries in 1971 with great success. By 1975, the population was robust enough to support harvesting, and the *C. gigas* "creuse" or "hollow" oyster became the ubiquitous half-shell oyster throughout France, with scores of regional variations available. The hardy *C. gigas* was capable of resuscitating the oyster industries of entire nations, and many countries gladly transitioned to the nonnative species.

Playing god with oyster species did not always have a happy outcome, however. In Australia and New Zealand, *C. gigas* quickly out-competed the valuable native rock oyster and became an invasive nuisance. Particularly in New Zealand, where the first *C. gigas* were suspected to have hitchhiked in ballast water, rock oyster populations were bullied into fringe habitat by the aggressive *C. gigas*. Australians—no strangers to the threat of nonnative invasives—began referring to the rapidly proliferating *C. gigas* oysters as "marine rabbits."[139]

The Russian-roulette introduction of *C. gigas*, with its checkered past as a sometimes-invasive species, could indeed come with a steep price. But as an international aquaculture juggernaut, its role as the savior of many a failed oyster fishery made it attractive to the desperate Chesapeake oyster industry. Setting aside its less-than-illustrious history in the Chesapeake (*C. gigas* was suspected as the original source for MSX in the Bay), it was considered for introduction to the Chesapeake as a way to restore the devastated oyster beds. Under a directive from the Virginia legislature, in 1998, VIMS began an extensive series of studies to look into the pros and cons of welcoming Asian oysters to the Bay. *C. gigas* was the first species on the list to be assessed.

The outcome of the experiments was lackluster. While *C. gigas* heartily resisted the virulent MSX and Dermo diseases without a problem, the environment of the Chesapeake proved to be less than ideal. It just wasn't salty enough. Also, *C. gigas* looked and tasted nothing like a Chesapeake oyster—a problem when consumers ordering a dozen Chesapeakes had very clear expectations about what it meant. The research for the perfect replacement continued.

Next to be considered was a Chinese species, *Crassostrea ariakensis*. There were a lot of things to like about *C. ariakensis* as an option for bolstering the Bay's native oyster stocks. *C. ariakensis* was resistant to MSX and Dermo and grew more quickly than the native *C. virginica* to a market size of three inches. It also filtered the water of algae and suspended sediment at an impressive rate. Plus, by all consumer tests, it was pretty tasty—an essential attribute.

Scientists urged caution and further study. *C. ariakensis* had some known drawbacks—a thinner shell, which made it more susceptible to predators; less hardiness in the low-oxygen conditions of the modern Chesapeake;

and a susceptibility to the Bay's nastier algae varieties. Other concerns were unknown. Did it grow in reefs or spread along the bottom? Could fishing and natural predators control the *C. ariakensis* population, or would it become an invasive nuisance like the Great Lakes' zebra mussel?

It was clear it would take intensive research to discover answers to these questions and understand the full ramifications of introducing *C. ariakensis* to the Chesapeake. Following the work at VIMS, a decade of thorough investigation began, undertaken by laboratories in Virginia and Maryland as well as the federal government. Starting with a *C. ariakensis* symposium hosted by VIMS in 2001, the process continued with a 2003 report by the National Research Council and culminated with a five-year study overseen by the U.S. Army Corps of Engineers to produce a comprehensive Environmental Impact Statement. It was a lengthy, if necessary, interlude in the race to find a remedy for the Chesapeake's oyster problem. But back in waterfront towns where groaning skipjacks mounded with oysters had reliably supported the winter economy for years, margins were tightening and expressions were growing grim.

For commercial watermen, the promise of a quick recovery of the once-mighty oyster industry was deeply appealing, and the benefits in swift action were clear. The years of cautious study were frustrating to people who watched their livelihoods dwindling each year as the oysters continued to die. In an interview on the Asian oyster, packinghouse owner and waterman Tucker Brown from Hollywood, Maryland, echoed the sentiments held by many working on the water: "It's fine oyster, but if we don't do something with it Maryland's out of the oyster industry. It's bad." His brother Robert Brown, a fellow waterman, concurred: "Doing nothing like we've been doing you see where that's gotten us. Bring it (the Asian oyster) on…the other oyster's just not doing it."[140]

It was an opinion that was shared by others in the industry, especially in Virginia, where the oyster leases as well as the wild harvest were hard hit. Larger oyster growers and packers, like Virginia's Bevans Oyster Company, were desperate to save their businesses. For them, Asian oysters might save not only their jobs but also all their employees at a family-run establishment that had been handed down for generations. The current situation made any investment in their disease-decimated industry futile. "We've been planting seed oysters in this river," said Ronnie Bevans. "When you plant oysters, it's like gambling, all the time—especially now. Since the mid-80s, the oysters have really started to decline. We have wonderful oyster bottoms in the Chesapeake and all its tributaries. It's a shame to have all this vacant bottom to be sitting there and not cultivated and put to use."[141]

Experimentation with Asian oysters would pay off in surprising ways. Initially, non-spawning oysters were used as a controlled way to study *C. ariakensis* by VIMS researcher Stan Allen, who had developed them in the 1970s during graduate school at the University of Maine. Reproducing oysters, known as "diploids," typically have two sets of chromosomes, but Allen discovered a way to encourage multiple sets of chromosomes in the Eastern oyster, *C. virginica*. By applying a chemical, cytochalasin B, during a critical moment in the oyster's cell development, Allen found he could produce an oyster with three sets of chromosomes. These triple-chromosome oysters, known as "triploids," are the molluscan equivalent of a mule—their odd number of chromosome sets stymie reproduction. This lack of fertility provides triploids a real advantage for several reasons. Triploids never divert any of their energy into reproduction, growing remarkably fast—a benefit in a lab environment. Plus their sterility makes them ideal controlled test subjects, without concern of any unintentional "escapes" of spat into the wild.

Allen refined his work further in the following years with the help of a Chinese researcher, Ximing Guo. Together, at Rutgers University, they developed a more stable way of creating triploids without chemicals after some chemically created sterile oysters reverted to reproducing diploids. By breeding a common diploid with a four-chromosome set "tetraploid," Allen would create the ideal subject for the Chesapeake's Asian oyster studies. These superior triploids, even when they came from nonnative species, could be planted in the Bay with little worry about subsequent generations of invasive spat absconding on the tide.

The public at large didn't quite know what to make of these non-reproducing oysters. A 2003 *Baltimore Sun* headline announced, "Oysters Deprived of a Sex Life: A Million Sterile Asian Bivalves Are to Be Introduced to the Bay to See How They Grow." The seafood industry, however, was hopeful. The executive director of the Virginia Seafood Council, Frances Porter, commented, "We are very determined to continue forward with this. It's good for our industry as we continue to develop our markets for the Asian oyster."[142]

Many watermen dismissed the concerns about the environmental implications of a nonnative oyster species and felt that the introduction of a diploid Asian oyster was the only sure-fire way to keep them in business. In a hearing on the Asian oyster in Cambridge, Maryland, Jim Kline of the Kent County Watermen's Association commented, "The greatest example of a non-native species is most of the people living today on the Eastern Shore—if non-native species are a threat to the Bay, they should be sending us back to England, where we came from."[143] Another waterman at the hearing agreed with Kline, likening Asian oysters to Sika deer, an introduced species thriving in the pine woods of southern Dorchester County: "Today in the marshes around Elliott, there are 100 sika for every 8 or 9 white-tailed natives and they are better eating than the white-tails."[144]

As the public debate continued, the research into *C. ariakensis* proceeded apace. Through his work with the newly created Aquaculture Genetics and Breeding Technology Center (ABC) at the Virginia Institute of Marine Science, Allen produced millions of *C. ariakensis* triploids to use in testing. He also created batches of native *C. virginica* triploids for use as a control group. Allen and ABC also recruited candidates familiar with oysters and bottom leasing that would be able to plant and observe bags of the two kinds of triploids: Virginia watermen. The watermen were trained in maintenance techniques for the oysters, which were grown in bags rather than fostered on the Bay's bottom in the manner of traditional oyster leases. As the trial concluded, the watermen made an unexpected discovery: both the *C. ariakensis* and the *C. virginica* were still alive and thriving.[145]

While the *C. ariakensis* survival was attributed to its hardiness in the face of MSX and Dermo, the *C. virginica* should have been dead, by all accounts. But it seemed that the sterile triploid had what Stan Allen refers to as "a turbo booster"—swift growth coupled with a powerhouse resistance to disease. The sterility of the *C. virginica* was a safeguard against MSX and Dermo. Typically, oyster diseases flourished in oysters weakened after reproduction. Triploid oysters never reproduced, so their resistance to the Bay's oyster scourges was at a constant high level. Their very sterility allowed the native triploids to reach market size before the ravages of disease killed them—a discovery of incredible impact.

The experiment proved that native *C. virginica* triploids—the Chesapeake's own species—could, through a chromosomal modification, be altered to circumvent the twin disasters sweeping through the wild oyster beds. By speeding up their growth and eliminating reproduction, the fear of an invasive species and the economic, environmental and market compromises entailed by moving to an Asian oyster could be completely avoided.[146] Customers could look forward to the sweetly salty Chesapeake oyster they'd grown up eating, and the environment could benefit from the native oyster's filtering and habitat. It was a watershed moment—both a pardon from a death sentence for the Bay's beleaguered oysters and a place for the Chesapeake's collapsed oyster industry to pin their hopes for the future.

Stan Allen agreed. Summarizing his findings, Allen stated, "Selectively breeding for a superoyster is absolutely the right thing to do, to enable aquaculture and commercial investment in the Bay. Oyster harvests in the Chesapeake Bay *will* be aquaculture in the future—I can think of multi-million dollar industries being based in the Bay. I'm mean, I'm an optimistic person, I peg all my optimism on aquaculture working. Oysters thrive in the Bay."[147]

Somewhere, William K. Brooks and the other aquaculture proponents of the nineteenth century were smiling.

While Allen's work would indeed pave the way for oyster farmers, the watermen who had so many hopes for their traditional way of life riding on the introduction of *C. ariakensis* were ultimately disappointed. In response to Allen's findings with the triploid native oysters, the Army Corps of Engineers concluded its study in 2009 with three recommendations for the future of the Chesapeake's oyster population and none involved introducing the Asian oyster. To restore the Chesapeake's oysters, the study endorsed redoubling efforts to restore the native oyster populations, enacting a harvesting moratorium, and utilizing non-spawning native oysters to expand native oyster aquaculture in the Chesapeake.

This coda would ultimately push Virginia's and Maryland's oyster industry in the direction that scientists like Allen had so long been advocating: aquaculture. But for watermen who saw the Asian oyster as a way to replenish the once-thick oyster reefs throughout the Chesapeake, the intensive cultivation of oyster farms were a mortal blow to their wild-harvest traditions. "What nobody wants to tell anybody is that it's not economically feasible," said Maryland Watermen's Association president Larry Simns. Cultivated oysters had to be grown in floats or cages, cleaned regularly and carefully maintained—techniques that were time-consuming and costly. They also grew from seed that had to be purchased from hatcheries. Simns continued, "If they were meant to be grown that way, they'd have airbags. There's a niche market for oysters grown by man, but it is not a practical way for today's watermen to make a living in the future."[148]

Simns had a point. The experiments with Asian oysters had also proven to be to be a testing ground for Virginia's fledgling oyster farmers—and the techniques developed by the partner watermen were indeed just that: farming, with all the painstaking work, equipment, financial investment and tending acreage that went along with it. It was a radical departure from Maryland's wild harvest approach and even for Virginia, which had some experience with oyster cultivation.

Unlike Virginia's traditional oyster leases, the triploids raised in the VIMS study were grown in cages, usually elevated off the bottom of the water. This allowed for easy maintenance, protection from predators,

Bottom cage oyster aquaculture on an oyster lease. *Photo by Jay Fleming.*

and observation of the oyster crops while bringing the oysters closer to the top of the water column, where more abundant algae and oxygen encouraged swift growth. It proved a successful precedent for the rest of the industry to follow, although there was still plenty of trial and error for leaseholders and entrepreneurs who wanted to follow aquaculture methods in the footsteps of the VIMS trials. Triploids may have represented the salvation of the Chesapeake's oyster industry, but that potential avenue for recovery was going to be painfully cobbled with major changes.

One of the greatest departures from the bottom-leasing techniques of Virginia's past was not the cages but the oysters themselves. Rather than the "broadcast" of wild spat from a naturally reproducing oyster bar—which also had the benefit of being free—watermen and oyster farmers were now totally reliant on labs and hatcheries for their triploid seed. Ranging between eight and twenty dollars per thousand depending on size, sourcing seed could be a costly affair, especially if you killed off several batches in the learning process. Referred to as "intensive culture," this technique used individual "seed" oysters that generally arrived in a clutch containing up to 1 million larvae for "single-oyster" rearing.[149] This produced a well-shaped oyster with a more rounded (or "cupped") interior shell, preferable for the higher priced half-shell market.

A second production method, "extensive culture," was developed a few years later to satisfy the shucking side of the Chesapeake oyster market. Intensive cultivation turned out a prettily shaped, appealing product. For the packinghouses around the Virginia Tidewater that had made their bread and butter on canning and shipping oysters, however, money talked louder than looks. Extensive (or remote setting) oyster growing meant that oyster farms could purchase their triploids already attached to old oyster shells. These spat-covered shells could be planted directly on oyster lease bottom, more like the traditional way, and grown in clusters that could be chipped apart with a culling hammer and shucked in the packinghouse. It was an economical approach that eliminated the need for expensive oyster cages and floats, as well as the time-consuming attention lavished on individual oysters in the intensive method.[150]

The oyster cultivation techniques developed over the next few years by Virginia scientists and entrepreneurs blew the door open on aquaculture in the state. From the time that Virginia's shellfish aquaculture began being tracked and measured by VIMS in 2006, triploid oyster cultivation soared. Hatchery-produced seed plantings grew from 6.2 million in 2005 to 138 million by 2014—an increase of over 2,125 percent in less than a decade.[151] But this transformation in the industry was not tallied just in oyster plantings. From individual watermen to the newly established triploid hatcheries, residents throughout Virginia's coastal communities were pulled by the flood tide of oyster cultivation.

Down at the very tip of Virginia's Eastern Shore, where the long, flat peninsula of land tapers to just a finger separating the Chesapeake from the Atlantic, is the Ballard Oyster and Fish Company, one of the success stories from the triploid's rapid ascendance. Headquartered in Cheriton, Virginia, Ballard has grow-out operations on both the Bay and ocean sides of Eastern Shore and boasts a line of no fewer than six kinds of oysters and four sizes of clams. Although today Ballard's docks are thick with the crushed spat shells from oyster cages and its upwellers foster millions of seed mollusks, the company's fortunes weren't always so bright.

Ballard's origins can be traced back to 1895, when a member of the Ballard family began working as a waterman harvesting oysters at the tail end of the oyster boom. Throughout the early twentieth century, the business was run as a wild oyster concern, the company building slowly as hundreds of additional oyster leases were purchased and cultivated. At one point, Ballard's oysters, shipped in their iconic blue-and-gold cans, could be found swimming in milky stews from Washington, D.C., to Chicago.

When MSX and Dermo began to impact Virginia's oyster population in the 1960s and '70s, Ballard's then-owner, Chad Ballard II, got creative. Transitioning the company's energies to the burgeoning hard-shell clam market, Ballard was reborn as the "Cherrystone Aqua Company," becoming internationally known for its meaty, sweet product. Ballard would only reenter the oyster market in the mid-'90s, when a longtime employee, Kenneth "Bubba" Frisby was given 100,000 spat with the directive: make them live.[152] Like many other Virginia newcomers to the uncharted waters of oyster farming, Bubba was able to improvise, and by the end of the year, 76,000 survived to make it to wholesale.

Today, Bubba's hard work has paid off. Ballard grows 10 million oysters a year—from the petite Chunus to the salty powerhouse Watch House Points, and it is in good company. Virginia's official roster of oyster aquaculture companies has more than four dozen listings, and this burgeoning industry is all pinned on the success of triploid oyster seed. Maryland, too, is beginning to enter the aquaculture market, complete with its own triploid spat sets. But it's been a much more tentative and contentious process than Virginia's sprint toward oyster farming.

In 2007, two years before the Army Corps of Engineers' report was released, Maryland had started to give its oyster industry a long, hard look via a taskforce, the Oyster Advisory Commission (OAC). The OAC, composed of scientists, watermen, anglers, economists and other Chesapeake stakeholders, was charged with advising the state on strategies for rebuilding and managing oysters in the Maryland side of the Chesapeake Bay.

The conclusion, released in 2009, was definitive and aggressive. Large portions of the Bay's productive oyster bars, the OAC report continued, should be put into restricted sanctuaries, where entire closed estuaries might be the focus of wild oyster restoration efforts. To further eliminate harvesting pressure on the Chesapeake's oyster population, the OAC recommended a complete transition of the state's wild oyster fishery into a privatized one based on aquaculture. This was a radical shift in the way Maryland thought about oyster restoration. In the past, scientists like William K. Brooks has advocated for the production of more oysters to improve the wild harvest. Now, OAC was telling the state to eliminate that harvest completely in exchange for a 100 percent farmed model.

Mark Luckenbach, a member of the commission, commented in a 2008 interview, "You cannot get away from the conclusion that any viable oyster industry has to be more based on aquaculture. Everywhere that has a completely wild fishery for oyster has collapsed, and every one of them managed to rehabilitate an industry did it based on increasing amount of privatizing and an increasing amount of aquaculture."[153]

The OAC's report, coupled with the recommendations of the Army Corps of Engineers, was the catalyst for swift, decisive action from Maryland's then-governor, Martin O'Malley. A democrat with an environmental bent, O'Malley announced his sweeping plan at the Annapolis Maritime Museum, formerly McNasby's Oyster Company. In it, he proposed to close several rivers to harvest, creating new sanctuaries, while opening 600,000 acres of the Bay's bottom to aquaculture. Scientists and conservation groups like the Chesapeake Bay Foundation were pleased—for many, the official state endorsement of aquaculture had involved decades of research and lobbying on their part. O'Malley, too, was optimistic about the environmental benefits for the beleaguered Bay. He also was hopeful that this public embrace of aquaculture would benefit not only new oyster farmers wanting to get into the business but watermen too.

The watermen, so eager only a few years ago for the rejuvenation of the wild oyster fishery the Asian oyster trials represented, did not see it that way. Maryland Watermen's Association president Larry Simns summed it up as a "disaster." Watermen were not farmers, and he perceived the capital investments required to get into aquaculture, like oyster seed, as well as the several years of work required before oyster reached legal size, as insurmountable obstacles. "They're forcing us out of one business and we're not ready to start on the other one," Simns said.[154] "They're saying they want to help the watermen with aquaculture, but the watermen, they know how to grow oysters," he continued. "And if it was going to be profitable they would be doing it. We're about making a living."

O'Malley's legislation paved the way for aquaculture by opening up enormous acres of Bay bottom, but it also attempted to address another long-time obstacle to would-be Maryland oyster farmers—untangling a snarl of county-specific regulations. In 2009, five Maryland counties had banned leasing entirely, and most others had a patchwork of restrictions and rules. Where leasing was allowed, oyster growers had to test their water for bacteria for twenty-four months and get a tidal wetland permit from the Board of Public Works and another tidal wetland license from the Army Corps of Engineers. The Department of Natural Resources and the Coast Guard also had to give their OK on any potential lease sites. And any waterman who contested the growing location could protest—which, more often than not, would be found in the waterman's favor. For most people interested in starting an oyster farm, it was enough to discourage them, or at least send them south to Virginia where the process was less onerous.[155]

O'Malley's vision called for a streamlined process that allowed lease applicants to only have to apply to the Maryland Department of Natural Resources for a permit, and in late 2010, the Army Corps of Engineers conceded to allow general permits for aquaculture—two changes that, in theory, shortened the waiting time for lease location approval to one year or less instead of sometimes more than two.

Slowly, applications started to come, first in a trickle and then in a flood. Although the permitting process was still arduous, the interest in growing oysters was blossoming. Submitted by entrepreneurs from all walks of life, from retired teachers and accountants looking for a change of pace to photographers, local young professionals and biologists, these were largely people who didn't fit the traditional waterman profile. A few from the waterman community did apply, too—some were "legacies," the children or grandchildren of working watermen who wanted a more stable way to get into the water business, or a handful of current watermen looking to make the switch. All of them hoped to capitalize on the newfound popularity of farm-raised oysters.

By 2013, there were thirteen oyster farms in Maryland, and over three hundred pending applications for new farms. It wasn't the explosive proliferation of Virginia, which boasted fifty-four farms by 2013, but showed a respectable expansion in a state that had only had one farm—Kevin McClarren's Choptank Oyster Company—just a few years before. Each of those thirteen oyster farmers were, by default, tenacious. Their permitting process had taken sometimes up to two years or more, and many of them had ongoing struggles with different groups who opposed their leases, whether nearby homeowners who worried over their water views or local watermen who protested the leases for infringing on other harvests like razor clams and crabs—especially water column leases, which reserved the use of the entire lease all the way to the top of the water for oyster floats or cages. The cultivation of triploid oysters was another concern—some of the public and watermen were uncomfortable with a lab-produced, non-spawning oyster.

A St. Mary's County waterman summed up the opposition to oyster farming in 2014:

*With aquaculture comes an oyster farming industry that wants large leases of water columns, not just bottom leases. These large water column leases prevent watermen from crabbing, fishing and other ventures that watermen do to earn a living. Floating and surface penetrating cages used by the oyster farmers for aquaculture create hazards for those that work or enjoy what mother nature has given us.*

*The Maryland State Waterman Association does not support such large water column leases. Property values are affected by the oyster farming industry. Property owners have little or no say about an industry being forced upon them virtually right in their backyard. It should also be mentioned that the oyster farms that only raise the triploid oyster is doing nothing to help restore the native oyster population! So all is not a good news story in oyster aquaculture even though the Maryland DNR and entrepreneur oyster farmers want to paint the picture as so.*[156]

Many of these objections were raised in public settings—in newspapers, on social media and in community forums. The Maryland Department of Natural Resources had built feedback and public commentary opportunities into the oyster lease permitting process, and often these became heated as oyster farmers, watermen, state officials and representatives from environmental groups spoke out on their respective positions. Often, the first oyster aquaculture applicant in a specific Maryland county, like Hollywood Oysters in Calvert County, would tackle the brunt of the initial opposition. Once their business was successfully established, other oyster farmers would follow, meeting much less opposition once the general community had accepted oyster farming on their river.

The focus of Maryland aquaculture moved from south to north. The southernmost tributaries, like the Patuxent River, were higher in salinity, and therefore provided a more stable environment for baby oysters to grow. That higher salt content also produced a saltier oyster—which, by common taste preferences, was a good thing. Aquaculture has been slower to develop in northern Maryland tributaries—indeed, by 2014, there were still viable rivers without a single oyster farm.

Plagued by recent influxes of freshwater from Hurricane Sandy and Irene, along with tropical storms, many of the Bay's northern rivers were less-than-ideal habitat for salt-loving oysters. The Chester River, a winding, forty-three-mile waterway bisecting Kent and Queen Anne's Counties, was a perfect example. Once rich with productive wild oyster shoals, the few bars that remained were scattered holdouts or the product of state spat-seeding initiatives. The river hadn't been a force in the oyster industry for several decades, and even local watermen from nearby Rock Hall tended to head south when oystering season opened. Scott Budden, the first oyster lease applicant on the Chester, hoped to change that. Putting in an application for a lease just north of Eastern Neck Island at the river's confluence with the Bay, he had dreams of producing an oyster renowned for its sweetness.

Budden is a Kent County, Maryland native who represents the new face of aquaculture—young, passionate, motivated and armed with investment capital and a business plan. Like many of the Eastern Shore's twenty- and thirty-something population, he moved away from his hometown of Chestertown, for college and then for career opportunities farther afield. Beyond farming or small business ownership, there just wasn't much of a professional incentive to return home. Personally, however, there were a million reasons—a close-knit community full of family and friends, a life lived close to the land, a slower pace, a beautiful landscape.

"I studied a little bit of aquaculture and environmental science in my undergrad studies, and it just seemed really interesting," Budden comments, opening up a small marine notebook full of salinity measurements and oyster cage winch plans. He continues, "In the back of my mind I thought, wouldn't that be really cool to try that in my hometown in the Chesapeake? And then when they passed the laws in 2009, all of a sudden, that idea came back, and I thought, I should look into this as a viable thing."

For Budden, it was more than a way to support himself—he saw oyster farms as an opportunity to resuscitate a Chester River imperiled by worsening water quality. "I saw it as a two-fold opportunity," Budden explains, "to make a living, but also to help clean up the Bay and river I grew up on and I love. I've seen it change a lot in my lifetime. When I was a kid, we used to go trotlining and catch huge crabs, way up in the river. Now, my friends will go out and catch one crab all day."

Budden spent the next three years getting his ducks in a row. He interviewed other oyster farms and observed their growing practices, researched different gear and improvised when he couldn't find exactly what he needed, took bottom soundings of different prospective locations along the Chester River looking for the ideal site: old shell bottom, good currents, a source of regular scouring from the Bay's main stem. He finally applied for the place he thought would be perfect—a location just north of the protected Eastern Neck Island, one of the places where thousand-year-old oyster middens clearly indicated that once oysters had thrived there.

Budden was optimistic. He had the gear he needed, he had a location identified that seemed prime for an oyster farm and he even started reaching out to people who might provide some part-time work to get the farm up and running. Then the lease went out for public comment. A routine part of the Maryland DNR leasing process, it allows different stakeholders to weigh in and voice concerns or obstacles. A waterman, Wayne Wilson, weighed in, protesting the lease. When DNR hosted a public open house on Budden's application, Wilson and a few other members of the Kent County Watermen's Association attended to share their opinions. Specifically, they objected to Budden's planned use of oyster cages, which they felt would foul other kinds of fishing gear like crab trotlines.

The Kent County commissioners, whom Budden had approached early on for their blessing and who had initially given him unanimous support, were now divided on the issue. One commissioner in particular, a former waterman himself, felt that that community needed an opportunity to discuss Budden's lease in a more public forum than a DNR hearing. The commissioners then added Budden's lease proposal to one of their meeting agendas in January.

It was a packed house—past standing room only, people trailed out into the lobby or leaned against the walls. Budden opened with a presentation on the lease, giving an overview of the process, his commitment to the region, the river and the local economy. He was followed by a long line of members of the public who all had plenty of opinions on the matter. There was support, from the local river association, from locals who admired his entrepreneurial spirit, from another oyster farmer—Johnny Shockley—a waterman turned oyster farmer who testified to Budden's thoroughness and the overall benefits of aquaculture.

"Really, we're in trouble with our seafood industry," Shockley stated. "We have to figure out what the future is going to be around this industry. This oyster aquaculture industry is the answer to all of these problems. I've jumped into this business because I want to create a way to carry on the heritage and future of the Chesapeake." Shockley spoke not only to the commissioners but also to the skeptical group of Chester River watermen:

> *The watermen here tonight I consider my peers—I would be very interested to see if in five years, how many of these same individuals are coming forth and asking for this same lease opportunity as aquaculture continues to flourish. We started out* [at Hoopers Island Oyster Aquaculture Company] *three years ago. This year, we'll be at $1.4 million. I'm supporting three other businesses right on Hooper's Island, employing twenty-five people. I see nothing but upside from this industry—to revolutionize seafood in the Chesapeake Bay.*

Then came the detractors. The landowners adjacent to Budden's lease had a lucrative waterfowling outfitters and guiding business on their property, and they were concerned that frequent boat trips to maintain oyster cages would disturb the birds. Budden's lease was only a few hundred yards from one of their several hunting blinds. Moreover, the landowners had good relationships with the local watermen and were worried that Budden's oyster cages would have a negative impact on their crabbing.

Next, a series of watermen voiced their concerns. Brian Nesspor, the vice-president of the Kent County Waterman's Association, summed up the general gist when he said, "You let this through, this one lease for these cages, it's going to lead to another one, and another one, and another one. Going right on up and down the shoreline. By a certain point in time, there is going to be no trotline bottom for these fellas when they have to go in four or five feet of water. It's going to be bottom that's once more taken away from the watermen that we'll never get back."

The meeting concluded tensely, with clutches of people divided along opinion lines congregating to discuss the matter in the parking lot outside. Although beyond the Chesapeake's tideline is technically all public property, supervised and managed by each state, many individuals still feel a strong sense of ownership and all the pride and entitlement that goes along with it.

In the following weeks, a mediator was called in to try to find some common ground between Budden, the adjacent property owners and the watermen. One of the terms agreed upon was that Budden would choose another lease site slightly south of the one he'd originally applied for. Located off Eastern Neck Island wildlife refuge, his only neighbors would be tundra swans and loblolly pines. The local delegate, Jay Jacobs, also a former waterman, promised to fast-track Budden's lease application in Annapolis if he shook hands on the deal. Budden agreed—just one concession among scores made in deals just like this around Maryland, as oyster farmers, watermen, property owners and recreational hunters all tried to navigate these new, worrisome waters of aquaculture.

Scott Budden's experience is not an isolated one. Conflicts continue to arise in Maryland over aquaculture and its new take on an old tradition, but cultivated oysters, and those who raise them, are still multiplying apace in Maryland and Virginia. Nationally, the United States is transitioning from an era of cheap, plentiful, processed foods into a period where regional flavors and sustainability rule the table. Oysters—a key component of that "slow food" trend—are once again flourishing in the Chesapeake's quiet coves as national demand grows for a cultivated product. Farmed, not wild, these

# THE OYSTER PALACE

Three dozen oysters on the half shell are served to the table at Pearl Dive. Pillowed by drifts of ice, their tender, gleaming insides are offered up seductively. In the restaurant's trendy dining room, where the décor shows a strong influence of Restoration Hardware, well-heeled city dwellers consume oysters in every conceivable fashion. Although they're bellying up for half-shells in Washington, D.C.—the heart of Chesapeake oyster country—their oysters hail from remote locales: Maple Point, Washington, Tatamagouche, Nova Scotia, East Dennis, Massachusetts. Pearl Dive's patrons are on a trip around the country, and they've never left the table. Each oyster manages to be a sea capsule, a tiny container cradling a teaspoonful of its home environment. The Washington oysters taste like cucumber, the Massachusetts are creamy and faintly coppery. One friend eating an oyster from the New Jersey shore, where he grew up, swears his tastes just like childhood summers spent swimming at the beach.

Oysters absorb and reflect their surroundings. Like wine, they are the delicate product of sun and minerals, weather patterns, location and climate. In the parlance of oenophiles, this is *terroir*—loosely translated as "a sense of place," *terroir* refers to the characteristics that the local environment has imbued on the region's wine. In the lingo of "ostreaphiles," or oyster connoisseurs, this quality is known as *merroir*—the same idea as *terroir*, just underwater. It is *merroir* that makes an oyster harvested off the Damariscotta

River taste crunchy with salt, but the same species taken from the Maryland side of the Chesapeake Bay has a languid sweetness with the faintest note of brine. Even oysters taken from different regions of the same body of water can taste dramatically different, as anyone who has compared oysters from the Chesapeake's Rappahannock and Chester Rivers knows.

Modern oyster raw bars embrace this desire to compare and contrast. Oysters are sourced from a dizzying array of national and often international locations. Carefully displayed on the restaurant's main floor in glacial little mountains of ice, consumers can select tiny Kumamotos from Japan or hulking monster *gigas* varieties from Washington State. There are no corners of the globe whose oysters are unappreciated in the oyster palaces of today. Lashed with a delicate mignonette or powdered with frozen granules of Tabasco, the raw oysters keep arriving in endless circular platters. Shells are upended as each is sipped from its jacket and consumed, and the only limit to the horizons of your palate is that defined by your credit card.

For the national's capitol, this revival of interest in oyster bars has a strong undercurrent of déjà vu. Perusing the photography collections at the Library of Congress, a snapshot in black and white taken just a few blocks away has perfectly preserved a bygone piece of Chesapeake culture: the Victorian oyster house. Shot on "Oyster Alley" near the corner of Pennsylvania Avenue and Twelfth Street, the sharp blacks and silvers of the 1922 image show three buildings in a row, competing for the city's oyster eaters. It is easy to see how appealing the painted signs on their gleaming plate windows would have been to the city's mustachioed bureaucrats. Listed in bold lettering, oysters were on offer in every conceivable way, from simple shucked oysters to oysters stewed, fried and steamed. Not unlike today's Pearl Dive, these establishments were watering holes for the city's white-collar workers after the workday. Seeking the remedy for a day's thirsty work, lawmakers and office workers would have washed down a couple dozen oysters with a few pints before lurching home, sated.

This scene was one replicated in almost every city and town throughout the United States. Oyster bars were a ubiquitous sight in the late nineteenth and early twentieth century. Regardless of the proximity to oyster-bearing waterways, as long as your town had railroads, the oyster cans regularly arrived by freight and restaurants were built to sell them. For almost two hundred years, oyster houses from Cripple Creek to Chicago peddled Chesapeake oysters in every recipe imaginable. They were part of the bountiful American diet, transported by progress, supplied by providence and processed by the great industrial machine.

In the second half of the last century, however, the oyster houses like those along "Oyster Alley" began to shutter throughout the Chesapeake and beyond. As the Bay's oyster populations plummeted and their prices rose, new kinds of cheap, internationally sourced seafood from king crab legs to fish sticks took their place. Beef and chicken production also became industrialized, replacing oysters as the inexpensive protein of the working classes. In the post–World War II era of Hungry Man dinners and efficient fast-food eateries, "old fashion" oyster saloons with their dark wood paneling and dim, smoky interiors seemed hopelessly outdated.

In the Chesapeake region, the demand for abundant, inexpensive blue crabs began to rapidly eclipse the remaining oyster market. Crabs were a symbol of the modern American summer. Widespread refrigeration and the new interstate highway system made what had previously been a local, perishable treat a classless cornerstone of the Chesapeake diet, ranging far beyond the Bay's boundaries. Watermen took advantage of the change in the market, with many transitioning to a summer-focused industry that utilized new gear, like the recently developed crab pot. With mallets in hand, the Bay's former oyster eaters demolished more piles of steamed crabs than ever before. Even the regional condiments changed to suit the crab's exploding popularity. In 1939, a recent immigrant to Baltimore from Nazi Germany, Gustav Brunn, developed a seafood spice he named after the Old Bay steamboat line. The distinctive mustard-yellow Old Bay can has been a staple of crab feasts ever since.

Unlike the quick, efficient protein of oysters, crabs were a food to be eaten at long leisure. Their delicate meat, contained within numerous little crannies inside the crab shell, requires a sharp knife and endless patience to prize out. In the past, crabs were too much work and too quickly perishable to be a significant part of the working-class diet. In the twentieth century, however, things changed. As the working classes around the Bay benefited from regulated workdays and mandatory weekends, the time it took to slowly deconstruct a bushel of blue crabs was blissfully free. Over hours at papered picnic tables with friends and conversation, accompanied with corn, tomatoes and pitchers of beer, eating crabs was more of a summer pastime than a way to fill a growling belly.

Development also encouraged the transition from oysters to crabs. In 1952, at either side of the newly constructed Chesapeake Bay Bridge, waterfront crab houses proliferated. These family-friendly establishments, with decks and picnic tables, were a convenient stopping point for summer traffic—now forgoing the Bay's traditional resort towns for the sugary beaches of the Atlantic coast. Within two generations, the transition from an oyster economy to a crab economy was complete. Chesapeake oysters had lost their position as the region's cheap, classless staple, becoming a luxury food served only in Thanksgiving stuffing or the occasional stew. The time of the oyster house was over.

The Chesapeake oyster's precipitous fall from popularity was to due to a complex combination of factors—environmental, cultural and economic. Oysters, beleaguered by disease, low market demand and the competitive crab harvest, had finally lost their position as the Bay's quintessential food. Unfortunately, the disappearance of the oyster in the environment and on plates was nothing new for the Chesapeake Bay. Sturgeon, shad and other delicious Bay species had all been fished to the edge of collapse, their historic habitat changed radically by human pressures. Like these once-mighty fisheries, oysters, too, seemed doomed to a future as a footnote in the region's history.

Although demand was lower than ever before, watermen, fewer each year, doggedly went out each winter in search of the Bay's ever-elusive oyster beds. But as the years went on, there were simply fewer people interested in eating them. Oyster prices were often too prohibitively expensive, and most folks forgot about the transcendent brine of the oyster's acquired taste after a generation or two. Once harvested, oysters were now typically destined for the packinghouse rather than the oyster house, where they'd be perfunctorily shucked and have their meats washed, packed and shipped. Consumers might include these "shucking market" oysters as an ingredient in a recipe, but they weren't savored raw anymore. And so the bliss of a dozen Chesapeake oysters, carrying the mineral tang of the Chesapeake's meandering byways, was lost to most for decades.

That might have been the end of the Chesapeake oyster's long chapter in the Bay's culture and foodways. But in just the last few years, there has been an unexpected oyster renaissance. Fomented by the explosion in popularity of the slow food and farm-to-table movements, the backlash against hyper-processed industrial foods has reawakened interest in American regional shellfish. Aided by scientific advances made in oyster disease resistance and oyster farming techniques, a new kind of oyster industry, and consumer, is emerging. Sold in upscale oyster houses like Washington, D.C.'s Pearl Dive, the new generation of Chesapeake shellfish is rigorously cultivated and marketed more like pearls than the humble organisms that create them. These oysters, lyrically named, are then marketed to well-heeled consumers with no qualms about spending four dollars for a perfect "Pleasure House" or "Ruby Salt." A new sun is rising over the Chesapeake's shellfish farms and the foodies who love them. For the Bay's beleaguered oyster industry, a brighter future is a tantalizing possibility—but only for those who can adapt to standards of this discerning new global market.

Julie Qui is the face of this modern oyster consumer, willing to plunk down a premium for the freshest, most vibrant oysters available. Her blog inahalfshell.com, Facebook page and Instagram account all feature gorgeously shot photos of her oyster-tasting trips to Ireland, Japan, China, the Pacific Northwest and the Chesapeake. Her website features guides, how-to's and recommendations on everything from shucking knives and drink pairings to the best places to find fresh oysters. In her hometown of New York City, Qui even leads tastings and classes to instruct initiates in the subtle art of oyster enjoyment. In short, Qui is a self-made oyster expert—and a recent one, at that. Admittedly, Qui has only had her "bivalve curiosity" since 2009. But perhaps that is fitting. Qui's passion for shellfish is only slightly younger than this American oyster renaissance. It's a whole new market, feeding the sort of informed, curious consumer that regularly haunts farmer's markets and considers the sustainability of their steak.

American oyster connoisseurship, therefore, isn't an entrenched old boy's club. This is a new area of expertise, populated, like Qui herself, by a younger crowd. Today's oyster aficionados are interested in the shellfish, certainly, but also in the subtleties and location of their production. They want to get their feet wet touring the oyster farms where their shellfish have been rigorously raised, and master the art of shucking their own oysters with finesse. The posterboy for this modern wave of oyster appreciation is author Rowan Jacobsen, whose 2008 book *A Geography of Oysters* was the first guide to getting up close and personal with shellfish. Conversational and to-the-point, with flavor profiles of regional oysters from around the world, Jacobsen sparked the interest in American oyster connoisseurship. Julie Qui herself was no exception to Jacobsen's infectious enthusiasm. Today, she refers to *A Geography of Oysters* as "her bible." "When I was first starting out," she explains, "I used to take it to oyster bars and use it as a tasting guide. He's my hero."

Early on in her quest to discover as much as she could about oysters, Qui took a trip to the West Coast, whose oyster industry is famous world over for its production of different kinds of shellfish, from native Olympia oysters to Kumamotos from Japan on huge tidal farms. A meal Qui describes as "all kinds of crazy oysters I had never seen before on the East Coast" at Hog Island Oyster Bar in San Francisco stirred Qui's budding oyster sensibilities.

Since then, Qui's interest in oysters has blossomed into self-professed obsession. In the last six years, she's sampled over three hundred varieties of oysters from six continents and fifteen countries. It's fair to say that as far as Julie Qui is concerned, oysters are more than just a passing food fancy.

Qui sees the growing popularity of oyster appreciation as part of the larger American shift in food production. A meaningful proportion of consumers are moving away from industrial convenience foods toward a burgeoning mindfulness about the sustainability, flavor and source of their diet. "I think it's gotten to a point where people are starting to see that it's not just about eating oysters—it's about getting that experience—something distinctive you can't get anywhere else. It's essentially the intersection between marketing and personal discovery."

For a generation preoccupied with defining its individualism while simultaneously reacting to the effects of food globalization, cultivating an interest in sustainable regional specialties is right on trend. Qui continues, "This kind of exploration is something that has been prominent across our generation, really for the past decade. A lot more emphasis has been placed on food, in a way the country has never seen before. In Europe, they've been doing this for a long time, but here it's just starting to catch on."

Although nationally the oyster industry is booming thanks to this new interest in farm-raised shellfish, nowhere is the power of the slow-food movement more evident than in Virginia. Here, where aquaculture is just starting to catch up to the established powerhouse shellfish farms in France, the Pacific Northwest and New England, oyster farms have explosively proliferated in the last decade. Hatchery-produced oyster plantings have multiplied in percentages in the thousands, and along the protected shorelines of the lower river systems, pipes or buoys marking bottom cages have become a common sight.[157] Most of these oysters are being grown through small- or medium-scale oyster farm ventures, with a few larger operations like Rappahannock River Oysters or Ballard Oyster Company. And all of them are competing for the custom of consumers like Julie Qui.

Qui remembers clearly her first real impression of the unique flavor profile of Chesapeake oysters: "Years ago in 2012, one oyster grower, Tommy Leggett, e-mailed me and asked me if he could send me some of his oysters. Of course I said yes, and he shipped up a box of York River oysters he grew. And I remember appreciating Chesapeake oysters for what they were. And they were different from what I experienced elsewhere. They were bigger, meatier, less briny, had this really interesting buttery robustness to them that you don't get in the Northeast."

Qui's lyrical description of Bay oysters might be surprising to those uninitiated in the world of oyster connoisseurship. They sound more appropriate for someone savoring a glass of fine wine than an oyster on the half shell. But oysters and wine have more in common than one might think. Oyster appreciation has borrowed a lot of ideas from the modern oenophile, from terminology to the development of regional characteristics like France's appellations.

Indeed, in Virginia in 2014, an official map of "oyster regions" was developed by the Artisan's Center of Virginia. It divided Virginia's waterways into seven areas, each with its own distinguishing flavor profile from the "sweetwater oyster with a light cream taste" of region four to the "initial bold saltiness mellowing into a sweet butter/cream finish" of region one. Echoing the existing Virginia wine trails, the regional map suggests activities and diversions along your oyster pilgrimage, from chats with local oyster farmers to tours of colonial plantations. For Virginia, oysters represent a natural offshoot of their heritage tourism program—from farm to fork, grape to glass and Bay to belly.

The parallels of Virginia's oyster farms and vineyards have been further celebrated in annual events pairing regional shellfish and wines like "Wine and Brine" or "Merroir and Terroir." These local tastings, promoted with the tagline, "What Grows Together, Goes Together," are often a far cry from traditional oyster celebrations. Contemporary oyster-and-wine tastings tend to appeal to a well-heeled sort of consumer happy to discuss the harmony of his or her Chardonnay and "heirloom oyster" pairing. In audience and overall feeling, however, they bear little resemblance to old-fashioned oyster events like Chincoteague's annual Oyster Festival or Maryland's St. Mary's County Oyster festival, where light beer, country music and wild oysters shucked packinghouse style still reign supreme. An echo of the days when oysters were a workingman's staple, these family-friendly events still take place year after year even as the ticket prices rise. Both kinds of oyster feasts celebrate the Bay's bivalves, but one might find its participants lingering over the merits of a half dozen, while at the other, it's shuck 'em, slurp 'em, get it done.

The revival of the Chesapeake's half-shell industry through oyster farms is changing the Bay's modern foodways and economy. Similar transformations are happening throughout the United States, with the East Coast seeing an especially pronounced expansion. Formerly productive oyster bars that were impacted by disease or, in the case of regions close to Boston or New York, fished out are once again producing shellfish as the bottom is leased and cultivated by oyster farmers. The East Coast Shellfish Grower's Association estimates that in the past five years alone, oyster production has doubled, with over one thousand small farms selling oysters under three hundred to four hundred oyster brands.[158]

This new generation of oyster brands is borrowing techniques well known to their nineteenth-century counterparts. Whereas in that era oyster cans boasted all sorts of suggestive imagery from Elvis to magicians to beautiful women, this generation has its own way to get a competitive edge. Names are given particular attention. Evocative and memorable, oyster brand names suggest delights from environmental to earthly: "Shooting Point Salts," "Witch Ducks," "Barren Island," "Forbidden," "Pleasure House." Often, one particular large producer like Rappahannock Oysters or Ballard will have several differently named brands, each catering to different tastes or price points.

It's a remarkable change for a place that used to produce only two kinds of oysters—Chesapeake and Chincoteague—and an indication of the national and global oyster market pressures Bay shellfish farmers face. In an industry where one oyster bar might boast twenty different varieties, name recognition for your individual line of oysters is crucial to winning consumers' hearts through their stomachs.

The battle for the loyalty of oyster lovers is taking place throughout the Chesapeake, but it's one crowded with national as well as regional competition. The Bay's small oyster farmers are vying not only against one another but also against aquaculture giants ranging far from the watershed. These large, established brands from the Pacific Northwest and New England hail from places where aquaculture is nothing new, and their mountains of fresh oysters crackling with salt and vitality provide formidable competition for the small start-up oyster farms from the Bay's rivers and coves.

The challenges faced by Chesapeake shellfish startups as they attempt to stake a claim in the "white tablecloth" market are exemplified by events like Washington, D.C.'s annual Oyster Riot. "Bacchanal" hardly conveys the decadence of this party, where rivers of champagne effervesce in sparkling glasses, waiting to be paired with a world's cornucopia of shellfish. Each year, hundreds attend, paying handsomely for the privilege of savoring the best of the best of a closely vetted selection of international oysters and fine wines. Since it's a Chesapeake event, you might assume local oysters would be well represented. But in 2013, only one brand managed to make the cut—a sobering reminder of just how far the local aquaculture industry has to go. To make it to the Oyster Riot, an oyster must be consistently delicious, consistently pure and produced in staggering numbers. These three goals might seem simple enough, but as any fledging oyster farmer will tell you, achieving them all at once is a feat nigh impossible.

A crowd trails out of the glass doors to the atrium at the Old Ebbitt Grill, even though the sidewalk is covered in trodden slush and temperatures hover at just under freezing. Most in the queue are well dressed, and a few sport boas and top hats—rather conservative attire even for the Oyster Riot's daytime spin-off event. The evening attendees will come clad in silks and satins of every color, adorned in finery meant to hide little and suggest even more. But it's just before noon at the so-called Quiet Riot, and so slightly more circumspection seems in order.

The old adage that "it's five o'clock somewhere" seems pretty universal once your tickets are punched and you enter the party. Faces and conversation are already warmed by the bonhomie magically found at the bottom of champagne bottles. Each guest upon arrival was handed a wine glass, to be refilled as often and copiously as they wish. But for most Oyster Riot participants, the wine is merely an accompaniment to the main act—endless tables piled high with crushed ice and thousands upon thousands of glistening oysters on the half shell. Shuckers culled from every oyster packinghouse and raw bar within two hundred miles are furiously cracking oysters, working hard to keep up the pace with the seemingly insatiable appetites of the Oyster Riot attendees.

Although oysters are on offer in every conceivable variation from sushi to stew, most Rioters are focused on the raw selections. With so many different varieties to compare, from acorn-sized Olympias to Edulis oysters as substantial as shoe soles, that makes sense. Cooking oysters tends to destroy their delicate marine essence, reducing them to a chewy, bland shadow of their former flavor. Even mignonette and cocktail sauce are little used here. Oyster Riot participants want to enjoy their oysters naked.

Unhindered by condiments, the flavor spectrum of the oysters available is incredible, ranging from the melon and cucumber notes of the Washington State Kumamotos to the creamy brine of the Massachusetts Wiannos. Each one is a totally unique sensory experience—and thanks to tireless quality control, there's not a bad one in the bunch. Yet only one, Battle Creek, is sourced locally.

Christian Guidi, a former manager of the Old Ebbitt Grill and a veteran of many Oyster Riots, is sitting at a table a little outside of the event's frenzied floor. He takes a break from selling merch emblazoned with the Riot's trademark mermaid to describe the Oyster Riot's selection process.

"We do a pretty extensive tasting—so for the twenty oysters or so that we have, we taste fifty, and we're very specific on size, presentation, and shell-shape," he says. "We also send the oysters to an independent lab for testing cleanliness and bacteria. It's a pretty rigorous selection process." He continues, "The other issue that we come into—we serve about three thousand oysters a day, we need the purveyors to be prepared to serve us at least five hundred oysters a day."

As the grand dame of D.C. oyster bars, and with the Oyster Riot increasing in local infamy, the Old Ebbitt Grill's standards for consistent excellence and volume have set the high bar for the regional white-tablecloth oyster market. "At first," Guidi explains, "we didn't have a lot of Chesapeake oysters because they couldn't commit to our standards. But independent of us, they've really become the market standards, for all these new oysters houses that have opened in D.C. in the last two or three years. So if Bay oysters want to make it, they have to step up."

In the Bay, where many aquaculture ventures are in their infancy, those standards represent dauntingly lofty goals, especially when most new farms are small, beginning with only five to ten acres under lease. Tim Devine, owner of the small but mighty Barren Island Oysters, knows these challenges only too well. His "slightly salty" oysters can be found in plenty of the Bay's high-end oyster bars, including D.C.'s Pearl Dive—surely a marker of success. But Devine readily admits that achievement was hardly the product of any kind of hard and fast plan. Like most of the Chesapeake's oyster farmers, he's just figured it out as he went along. Finding ways to grow as many perfect oysters as possible has taken a lot of ingenuity, experimentation and hard work. Most importantly, it's also taken Devine's stubborn conviction that if it's possible to produce the best-cultivated oyster in the Chesapeake, he's going to do it.

"The way I've always done things is to take my weaknesses and make them my strengths," Devine says. It didn't faze him that he knew nothing about growing oysters. As a native of Maryland's Eastern Shore turned New York photographer turned prodigal son returned, he's had plenty of opportunities to reinvent himself—a useful attribute when seeking to plunge into a career in oyster farming. The wide-open newness of the industry in the Chesapeake appealed to him. Devine continues, "All these other people in the business were coming from some sort of tradition. I don't have that, so I'm not going to be boxed in by anything. So, I could look at growing oysters with fresh eyes. I really allowed myself the chance to fail at this business."

A trip down to Devine's business on Hooper's Island clearly shows he hasn't failed—indeed, things are thriving for Barren Island Oysters. The cinderblock building hums with the activity of prepping cage after cage of oysters for shipment all around the region. It's the week before Superbowl Sunday, and several thousand of Barren Island's finest are headed out to share table space with buffalo wings and nachos during the big game. Several men in bibs and sweaters pile remarkably clean, well-shaped oysters on a conveyor belt to be sorted into boxes. Tim and his crew have worked hard to prepare his oysters, "BIOs" for short, for this moment. Like many oyster growers competing for a piece of the half-shell market, each individual oyster has been invested with months of rigorous cultivation.

Devine and his crew dedicate hours every week to tending their oyster crop. Each oyster cage must be regularly shaken to remove built-up algae and sediment, and individual oysters are also sent on a few trips through the large industrial tumbler. Pricey but essential for many oyster farmers, tumblers allow culitvators to "finish" their product in large rotating drums that toss the oysters around and chip off the fingernail-fine edges of their bills. Aquaculturists claim that this creates an oyster with a deeper interior "cup," less rough edges and, over time, a thicker shell free of barnacles and other reef animals. It's a time consuming and laborious step, requiring oyster farmers to move their oysters from the lease site to the tumbler and back multiple times. But tumbling and other cultivation techniques are necessity when the expectation of consumers is for oyster shells to be as pleasing to the eye as the meat is to the palate.

If tumbling provides an edge, many oyster farmers are willing to swallow the cost and extra work it entails. Stakes are high for Chesapeake oyster farms to produce ever more, ever better oysters to meet the upscale industry's demands. However, excellence and volume are hard to achieve simultaneously—a fact Devine readily acknowledges. "There are a lot of hurdles for Maryland oyster farmers at this early stage. The real problem is manpower and time. Finding labor in these rural places where you see oyster farms is really hard." Tim continues, "You have to put the time in. You don't have enough in the day to get the sediment, the growth of things that block water flow off—you really have break that up consistently, shaking them, turning them so they get better current, better algae."

Devine hopes to find a happy medium for his Barren Island Oysters between quality and quantity—a difficulty, when more intensive cultivation produces a better oyster but can limit the amount of shellfish a farmer can grow. It's a delicate balance, and it's relative. Each individual oyster grower has to identify how many oysters to plant and how much work to invest in each individual shellfish. Some cultivators may skimp a bit on manual processes, like tumbling, in favor of a larger crop. Others, like Tim Devine, will sacrifice a bit of their production quantity to get smoothly tumbled, buttery oysters.

After several years of trial, error and painstaking detail, Devine thinks his BIOs may have final found their equilibrium. This summer, barring any unforeseen circumstances like ice events or freshwater flooding, his Barren Island Oysters are poised to be ready for market in larger numbers than ever before. "I pushed it this year—put in 3.5 million. If the losses are what I expect, then this year, in June, I can bring 250 to 300 boxes—that's 25,000 to 30,000 oysters a week. It's set up to be consistent, producing that much from then on." With that kind of production, Devine's BIO brand would be well positioned to apply as a vendor at big events like the Oyster Riot, where they might win over the hearts (and palates) of oyster consumers and chefs alike.

For the Chesapeake's oyster farmers, investing hours of toil in the quality of their oysters is only the first step. Once they're ready for market, you need hungry mouths to consume all these shellfish—and winning over the loyalties of the region's oyster lovers is a tricky business. Oyster growers face stiff competition in their rapidly crowding field, pushing many farmers to look for creative ways to distinguish their brand. In Devine's case, that meant literally knocking on the doors of restaurants to persuade chefs to try his product. His pavement-pounding campaign was successful, garnering some contracts with popular restaurants, but Devine didn't stop there. He spent weeks strategizing BIOs' distinctive, eye-catching branding. "When I started out, everything was covered in anchors," Devine says, referring to the logos of his Chesapeake competition. "I saw a lot of room for improvement. I worked in New York, in that visual world for fifteen years, and I knew the importance the right box color and the right fonts could have."

Tim's distinctive blue logo with its line-drawn oyster is all over the BIO headquarters, on everything from oyster boxes to trucker hats (available for purchase at the low price of twenty dollars). He's worked hard to make sure that his oysters are memorable for their flavor and their brand's visibility. Devine's not above using humor, either. His "Ugly" line of oysters, an untumbled variety, boasts the tagline: "They've Got Great Personalities."

The kind of attention to detail lavished on Barren Island Oyster's marketing is starting to catch on, especially among the Chesapeake's bigger oyster farms. Many are run by Generation X and Y business owners, who have grown up online and feel comfortable harnessing the power of websites, Facebook, Instagram and Twitter for their brand's benefit. They also inherently understand the advantage that good design provides—a throwback to the turn of the century, when their predecessors at hundreds of oyster packinghouses competed for the loyalty of customers by creating beautiful, elaborate oyster cans.

Marketing isn't the only route to consumers' hearts. Some larger oyster farmers are seeking an even more direct approach to their would-be consumers. Especially in Virginia, shellfish cultivators are hoping to inspire an affinity for their brands by encouraging consumers and cooks to actually come down and see where their oysters are being grown. Like land-based agritourism, these oyster tours allow an up-close-and-personal look at the cultivation process, surrounded by the verdant beauty of the Chesapeake's salt marshes. Copious oyster sampling is, of course, part of the process. Again, oyster farmers take a cue from the wine world, where vineyards have long embraced the desire of the consumer to enjoy the environment that produced the wine they drink.

Chesapeake oyster tourism provides opportunities to get complete immersion in the merroir conveyed by a region's oysters—boots in the water, one might say. At Pleasure House Oysters on the Lynnhaven River, visitors on oyster farm tours can enjoy a farm-to-table experience where the distance between the two is less than two feet. Tour participants can arrange to have a table fashioned out of oyster cages set up in the river itself. Oysters are then brought out by the bushel and shucked for the hungry and, hopefully, newly appreciative crowd. Anderson's Neck Oyster Farms, located on the upper York River, offers an experience that explores the seemingly endless relationship between oysters and wine. On its six-hour Oyster Wine tour, participants visit two local vineyards before taking a jet boat to the oyster grow-out location for a tasting.

The world of oyster farming, it's clear, has a sensibility far removed from the traditional wild oystering industry, though the two are similar in their unglamorous realities. Both wild harvesting and oyster farming require backbreaking manual labor during the windiest or iciest Chesapeake days. Oyster farmers and watermen will be covered in bottom mud, head to toe, by the end of the day. To get a decent harvest, they'll cull through mud crabs and gobies, globules of sea squirts and the rank shells of dead oysters. Both watermen and oyster farmers will watch the sun rise while they're already at work and fall asleep early, sometimes at the dinner table. Bringing an oyster to market is no small feat, regardless of the method. But increasingly, the method, especially for raw oysters, is farming.

Without a doubt, the market for farm-raised oysters is booming, and restaurants and their patrons are clamoring for fresh, meticulously cultivated shellfish. What remains to be seen is how much of this trend is here to stay and how much is a passing fad. Proponents of the locavore lifestyle—the food movement behind this generational interest in local, sustainable ingredients—hope it represents a shift in culture rather than a passing fancy. Julie Qui is optimistic: "I think I would personally pay a premium to be able to know exactly where my oyster comes from and who grows it. It's important to me that I can see that line—from where it's planted, how it's being raised, to how it ends up on my plate. That is valuable, because having transparency in a food that you have to consume raw can address the risk."

Of course, as an oyster connoisseur, Qui understands the allure of farm-raised oysters goes beyond pragmatic concerns about cleanliness.

"Having a connection to whomever is making your food is powerful," she continues, "and this is one really effective way to be mindful about what you're eating. More people are interested in that kind of consumerism, but it has to have meaning, it has to be authentic—it has to go past names and marketing fluff. I really hope it's not a trend because, you know, oysters are awesome."

Many of the Bay's oyster farmers are banking on that awesomeness, hoping that as long as their products get in front of oyster eaters, the crisp brine and immaculate shell will do the rest of the work. Their futures, and that of the Chesapeake's fledgling cultivated oyster industry, are in the consumer's hands but more importantly on their plates, offered up as a dozen small mouthfuls of the Bay's essence.

In today's new oyster economy, this consumer power is paramount, for both oyster farmers and wild harvesters alike. The powerful connection Qui describes between the food we eat and our appreciation for its origins is the key. How and where you spend your money, whether on a waterman's wild-caught bushel or a one-hundred-count of the finest farmed oysters, shapes the future of the Chesapeake oyster industry even as it conveys your personal values. Yet so many consumers are still unaware they even have a choice.

"Chesapeake oysters" are no longer one kind of oyster but many kinds, from scores of farms and wild bars throughout Maryland and Virginia. A purchase of one brand or one region's oysters directly sustains that business. Therefore, the responsibility lies within each person who sharpens their shucking knife every fall, or who thinks nothing of plowing through several dozen at a sitting, to make an informed decision. Every barbecued, frittered, or raw oyster is a vote—for a Bay where watermen still leave the harbor, one where oyster farms are ascendant or somewhere in between. Never has there been such a meaningful, delicious opportunity to determine the next chapter for the Chesapeake oyster—the Bay's foundation and future.

# ACKNOWLEDGEMENTS

This book has been the product of tremendous generosity from Chesapeake colleagues and experts. I would like to thank Gordy Allen and Jay Fleming for their beautiful artistic and photographic contributions to this book. I would also like to thank Pete Lesher and the Chesapeake Bay Maritime Museum, Scott Budden, Tim Devine, Mark Connolly, Jane Cox, Danny Schmidt and Historic Jamestowne, Frank Clark and Colonial Williamsburg, Julie Qui, Dr. Stanford Allen and the Virginia Institute of Marine Science, Don Webster, Kathy Thornton and Rod Cofield and Historic London Town and Gardens for their contributions and expertise. I would like to also thank Bill Thompson, Rona Kobell, Nancy Robson and Adam Goodheart for their encouragement, editorial advice and just plain friendship. To my family and friends, thank you for enduring my endless oyster talk and supporting me along the way. And finally, to my commissioning editor, Hannah Cassilly, thank you for your guidance and professionalism—you've made me a better writer.

# NOTES

## CHAPTER 2

1. Wesley Frank Crave, *Dissolution of the Virginia Company* (Gloucester, MA: Peter Smith, 1964).
2. Arthur Barlowe, *The First Voyage to Roanoke, 1584* (Boston: Directors of the Old South Work, 1898).
3. John Smith, *The Generall Historie of Virginia, New England & the Summer Isles, Together with the True Travels, Adventures and Observations, and a Sea Grammar* (London, 1624).
4. Ibid.
5. George Percy, *Discourse of the Plantation of the Southern Colony in Virginia by the English, 1606* (London, 1608).
6. Ibid.
7. David A. Price, *Love and Hate in Jamestown: John Smith, Pocahontas, and the Heart of a New Nation* (New York: Alfred A. Knopf, 2005).
8. Smith, *Generall Historie*.
9. Daniel Schmidt and Dexter Haven, "A Pilot Study on the Origins of Oysters at James Fort," *Journal of the Jamestown Rediscovery Center* 2 (January 2004).
10. Williams Symonds, "The Proceedings of the English Colonie in Virginia. 1612," reprinted in *The Complete Works of Captain John Smith*, ed. Philip L. Barbour (Chapel Hill: University of North Carolina Press, 1986), 1:251–2.

11. Dr. Joanne Bowen and Susan Trevarthen Andrews, "The Starving Time at Jamestown: Faunal Analysis of Pit 1, Pit 3, the Bulwark Ditch, Ditch 6, Ditch 7, and Midden 1," Jamestown Rediscovery, scientific report, Association for the Preservation of Virginia Antiquities, October 2000.
12. Percy, *Discourse of the Plantation*.
13. Joseph Stromberg, "Starving Settlers in Jamestown Colony Resorted to Cannibalism," Smithsonian.com, April 30, 2013.
14. Percy, *Discourse of the Plantation*.
15. Schmidt and Haven, "A Pilot Study."
16. Percy, *Discourse of the Plantation*.

# CHAPTER 3

17. King James, *His Counterblast to Tobacco* (London: Printed for J. Hancock, 1672), Accession GT3020 .J35 1672a, Special Collections, Library of Virginia, Richmond, Virginia.
18. Lois Green Carr, Russell R. Menard and Lorena S. Walsh, *Robert Cole's World: Agriculture and Society in Early Maryland* (Chapel Hill: University of North Carolina Press for the Institute of Early American History and Culture, 1991).
19. Lois Green Carr, "The Metropolis of Maryland: A Comment on Town Development Along the Tobacco Coast," *Maryland Historical Magazine* 69 (1974): 124–45.
20. *Archives of Maryland LIII, Proceedings of the County Court of Charles County, 1658–1666 and Manor Court of St. Clements Manor 1659–1672, Court Series*, ed. J. Hall Pleasants (Baltimore: Maryland Historical Society, 1936).
21. James Horn, "Servant Emigration to the Chesapeake in the Seventeenth Century," *The Chesapeake in the Seventeenth Century: Essays on Anglo-American Society*, eds. T.W. Tate and D.L. Ammerman (Chapel Hill: University of North Carolina Press, 1979): 51–95.
22. James Horn, *Adapting to a New World: English Society in the Seventeenth-Century Chesapeake* (Chapel Hill: University of North Carolina Press for the Institute of Early American History and Culture, 1994): chapters 1 and 2.
23. Lorena S. Walsh, "Slave Life, Slave Society, and Tobacco Production in the Tidewater Chesapeake," *Cultivation and Culture: Labor and the Shaping of Slave Life in the Americas.* Carter G. Woodson Institute Series in Black Studies, University Press of Virginia, 1993.

24. Scott Tucker, "Canoes as Mechanisms of Social Identity and Resistance Amongst African-American Slaves in the Chesapeake" (master's thesis, University of Southampton, 2009).

25. Walsh, "Slave Life."

26. Ibid.

27. Alphonse Adite, Stanislas Sonon and Ghelus Gbedjissi, "Feeding ecology of the mangrove oyster, *Crassostrea gasar* in traditional farming at the coastal zone of Benin, West Africa." Scientific report, Université d'Abomey-Calavi, Cotonou, Bénin, 2013.

28. Ivor Noel Hume, "The Oyster's Tale," *Colonial Williamsburg Journal* (Summer 2003).

29. John Michael Vlach, *Back of the Big House: The Architecture of Plantation Slavery* (Chapel Hill: University of North Carolina Press, 1993).

30. Philip D. Morgan, *Slave Counterpoint: Black Culture in the Eighteenth-Century Chesapeake & Lowcountry* (Chapel Hill: University of North Carolina Press, 1998).

31. Miller, HM. "Transforming a 'Splendid and Delightsome Land': Colonists and Ecological Change in the Chesapeake, 1607–1820," *Journal of the Washington Academy of Sciences* 76 (1986).

32. Wm. J. Hinke, ed., "Report of the Journey of Francis Louis Michel from Berne, Switzerland, to Virginia, October 2, 1701–December 1, 1702," *Virginia Magazine of History and Biography* 24, no. 11 (January 1916).

33. Landon Carter, "Diary of Col. Landon Carter," *William and Mary Quarterly* 21, no. 3 (January 1913): 172–81.

34. Miller, "Transforming a 'Splendid and Delightsome Land.'"

35. Carter, "Diary."

36. George Washington, *The Writings of George Washington*, ed. J.C. Fitzpatrick (Washington, D.C.: George Washington Bicentennial Commission, US Congress, 1944), 39 vols.

37. Sharon V. Salinger, *Taverns and Drinking in Early America* (Baltimore, MD: Johns Hopkins University Press, 2002).

38. Ben Ford, "Wooden Shipbuilding in Maryland Prior to the Mid-19th Century," *American Neptune* 62, no. 1 (2002): 61–90.

# Chapter 4

39. James T. Lemon, "Colonial America in the 18th Century" in *North America: The Historical Geography of a Changing Continent*, eds. Robert D. Mitchell and Paul A. Groves (Totowa, NJ: Rowman and Littlefield, 1987): 121–46.

40. Sherry H. Olson, *Baltimore: The Building of an American City* (Baltimore, MD: Johns Hopkins University Press, 1980).

41. John M. Kochiss, *Oystering from New York to Boston* (Middletown, CT: Wesleyan University Press, 1974).

42. Tim Visel, Tessa Getchis and Peg Van Patten, "A Brief History of Connecticut Shellfishing" *Wracklines* (Connecticut Sea Grant publications) 14, no. 1 (Spring/Summer 2014).

43. Kochiss, *Oystering*.

44. Linda Breisch and Victor S. Kennedy, "Sixteen Decades of Political Management of the Oyster Fishery in Maryland's Chesapeake Bay," *Journal of Environmental Management* 164 (1983): 153–71.

45. "Maryland on a Half Shell," Underbelly, http://www.mdhs.org/underbelly/2014/05/08/maryland-on-a-half-shell/, May 8, 2014.

46. Ernest Ingersoll, *The Oyster Industry* (Washington, D.C.: U.S. Government Printing Office, 1881).

47. R. Lee Burton Jr., *Canneries of the Eastern Shore* (Centreville, MD: Tidewater Publishers, 1986).

48. Thomas Weeks, ed., *Industrial Statistics and Information of Maryland, 1884* (Baltimore, MD: Guggenheim, Weil & Co, 1886).

49. Lara Lutz, "Baltimore Museum of Industry Shows City Can-Do Spirit," *Chesapeake Bay Journal*, March 1, 2009.

50. Salomon Frederik van Oss, *American Railroads and British Investors* (London: Effingham Wilson & Co., 1893).

51. Charles Perry, "As American as Roast Oysters," *Los Angeles Times*, December 26, 2001.

52. Hugh S. Orem, "Baltimore: Master of Canning," in *A History of the Canning Industry and Its Prominent Men*, ed. Aurth I Judge (Baltimore, MD: Annual Convention of the National Canner's Association, 1914).

# CHAPTER 5

53. John R. Wennersten, "John W. Crisfield and Civil War Politics in Maryland," *Maryland Historical Magazine* 99, no. 1 (Spring 2004).

54. Woodrow T. Wilson, *History of Crisfield and Surrounding Areas of Maryland's Eastern Shore* (Baltimore, MD: Gateway Press, 1973).

55. *New York Times,* "Raising Oysters and Figs; Curious Farming Underway at Tangier Sound," January 15, 1893.

56. George Brown Goode, *The Fisheries and Fishery Industries of the United States* (Washington, D.C.: U.S. Government Printing Office, 1887).

57. *New York Tribune*, "The Oyster Trade. Second Letter. Statistics of the Chesapeake Oyster Trade the Oyster Packing Trade Oyster Culture in France the Oyster's Enemies, Etc.," March 27, 1869.

58. Richard S. Dodds and Pete Lesher, *A Heritage in Wood* (St. Michaels, MD: Chesapeake Bay Maritime Museum, 1992).

59. *Washington Post*, "Dredgers Hard Life: Rough Existence Led by Men on the Oyster Boats," December 8, 1901.

60. Ibid.

61. *Washington Post*, "Making Slaves of Men: Three Cruel Captains of Oyster Schooners Punished," April 2, 1889.

62. *New York Tribune*, "The Oyster Trade."

63. Ibid.

64. Hunter Davidson, *Report on the Oyster Resources of Maryland* (Annapolis, MD: WM Thompson, Printer, 1870).

65. John R. Wennersten, *The Oyster Wars of the Chesapeake Bay* (Centreville, MD: Tidewater Publishers, 1981).

66. *New York Herald*, "Bold Oyster Pirates," November 27, 1888.

67. Ibid.

68. *Baltimore Sun*, "The Oyster Question. Howitzers Ordered," November 28, 1888.

69. *New York Times*, November 28, December 8, December 12, 1888.

70. *New York Times*, "Maryland's Oyster War: Captain Howard's Story of the Battle of Monday," December 13, 1888.

71. Wennersten, *The Oyster Wars.*

72. Ibid.

73. *Baltimore Sun*, "The Oyster War," September 16, 1874.

74. Thomas Morrisett, "The Oyster Industry: It Needs Protection or It Will Soon Become a Lost Art," *Washington Post*, January 26, 1890.

75. *Baltimore Sun*, "Oyster Industry Failing," September 12, 1901.

# CHAPTER 6

76. Norman H. Plummer, *Maryland's Oyster Navy: The First Fifty Years* (Chestertown, MD: Washington College, Literary House Press for the Chesapeake Bay Maritime Museum, 1993).

77. Breisch and Kennedy, "Sixteen Decades of Political Management," 153–71.

78. Michael W. Fincham, "The Oyster Dreams of William K. Brooks," *Chesapeake Quarterly* (April 2013).
79. Edwin Grant Conklin, "A Biographical Memoir of William K. Brooks," Biographical memoirs series, part of vol. 7 (Washington, D.C.: National Academy of Sciences, 1913).
80. Fincham, "The Oyster Dreams of William K. Brooks."
81. Christine Keiner, *The Oyster Question: Scientists, Watermen and the Chesapeake Bay* (Athens: University of Georgia Press, 2009).
82. Ibid.
83. *Washington Post*, "The Oyster Question," September 3, 1905.
84. *Baltimore Sun*, "New Oyster Bill Is Intended to Promote Planting in Maryland," March 19, 1900.
85. George D. Santopietro and Leonard A. Shabman, "Common Property Rights in Fish and Water Quality: The Oyster Fishery of the Chesapeake Bay," scientific report, Duke University, 1990.
86. *Baltimore American*, "The Truth Which Hurts," January 24, 1903.
87. Pete Lesher, "Rented Bottom: Oyster Leaseholds on the Chesapeake Bay," *Weather Gauge* 32 (Fall 1996): 24–27.
88. Donald Webster, "Industry Training Pamphlet," University of Maryland, November 2007.
89. *Washington Post*, "Defend Oyster Beds: Strong Opposition in a Capitalistic Scheme," February 3, 1897.
90. *Washington Post*, "Farming the Oyster: September's 'R' Month Makes the Silent Bivalve Popular," August 18, 1895.
91. Lesher, "Rented Bottom."

# Chapter 7

92. "Chesapeake Bay Oyster Landings by State, 1880–2011," NOAA Fish Facts—Oysters, http://chesapeakebay.noaa.gov/fish-facts/oysters.
93. Dodds and Lesher, *Heritage in Wood*.
94. "Population History of Baltimore." U.S. Census Bureau, Washington, D.C.: GPO, 2015.
95. *Baltimore News*, July 16, 1897.
96. Christopher G. Boone, "Obstacles to Infrastructure Provision: The Struggle to Build Comprehensive Sewer Works in Baltimore," *Historical Geography Journal* (2003).
97. Ibid.

98. Breisch and Kennedy, "Sixteen Decades," 153–71.

99. Ibid.

100. Transcript, Paul Kellam oral history interview, December 12, 2013, by Ashley Bernatchez, Southern Maryland Documentation Project, St. Mary's College of Maryland Archives, http://smcm.cdmhost.com/cdm/singleitem/collection/p4105coll5/id/166/rec/2.

101. Ibid.

102. Tom Philpott, "A Brief History of Our Deadly Nitrogen Fertilizer," *Mother Jones*, April 19, 2013.

103. DATA SOURCE: National Marine Fisheries Service, http://www.st.nmfs.noaa.gov/commercial-fisheries/commercial-landings/annual-landings/.

104. Garrett Power, "More About Oysters Than You Wanted to Know," *Maryland Law Review* 30, no. 3 (1970).

105. Ibid.

106. Peggy Mullen Stull, "Tell Us Your Flood Stories," *Transformation from Tragedy, Survivors Remember the Flood of 1972*, oral history project, Community Foundation of Elmira-Corning, October 4, 2010.

107. Kent Mountford, "Agnes' Impact Still Haunts Parts of the Chesapeake 40 Years Later," *Chesapeake Bay Journal*, August 1, 2012.

108. "The Effects of Tropical Storm Agnes on the Chesapeake Bay Estuarine System," scientific report, Chesapeake Research Consortium, Inc. Johns Hopkins University Press, November 1976.

109. *Southern Maryland News*, "Share Your History: Working the Land, Water in Southern Maryland," September 26, 2012.

110. William G. Thomas, "The Chesapeake Bay," *Southern Spaces Journal* (April 2004).

111. Jack Greer, "Twenty Years After: Our Changing Vision for the Chesapeake," *Chesapeake Quarterly* 1, no. 1 (2002).

112. Merrill Leffler, "Don Meritt: The Hatchery Connection." *Chesapeake Quarterly* 1, no. 3 (2002).

113. Roger I.E. Newell, "Ecological Changes in the Chesapeake Bay: Are They the Result of Overharvesting the American Oyster, *Crassostrea virginica*?" scientific paper, University of Maryland, Horn Point Environmental Laboratories, March 1988.

114. Karl Blankenship, "New Study Suggests Oysters Could Reduce Nutrient Levels in Bay," *Chesapeake Bay Journal*, September 1, 2002.

115. Kent Mountford, "It's Called a Crab Jubilee, but the Crabs Aren't Happy and We Shouldn't Be," *Chesapeake Bay Journal*, September 1, 2008.

116. Allison Stuebe, "Praying for Rain in the Bay," *Washington Post,* July 13, 1995.

117. "Maryland Oyster Roundtable Action Plan," State of Maryland, December 1993.

118. Rona Kobell and Greg Garland, "Oystermen Reap Federal Bounty," *Baltimore Sun*, April 1, 2007.

119. Ibid.

120. Ibid.

121. Michael Fincham, "Homegrown Oysters, Homegrown Activists," *Chesapeake Quarterly* 9, no. 2.

122. Tom Horton, "Increase in Harvest an Oyster Shell Game," *Baltimore Sun,* February 25, 2005.

123. Transcript, Public hearing for Maryland Oyster Restoration and Aquaculture Development, Maryland Department of Natural resources, July 7, 2010.

124. Ibid.

125. Ibid.

126. Tim Wheeler, "O'Malley Plans to Limit Oyster Harvest," *Baltimore Sun*, December 4, 2009.

127. Ibid.

128. Karl Blankenship, "Maryland Getting Florida Oyster Shell to Build Reef," *Chesapeake Bay Journal*, December 19, 2013.

129. "Watermen Protest Maryland Oyster Project in Dorchester County," www.wboc.com, May 1, 2014.

130. Jonathan Wilson, "How a Maryland Hatchery Is Helping Chesapeake Bay Oysters," WAMU.org, March 27, 2015.

## CHAPTER 8

131. John W. Ewart and Susan F. Ford, "History and Impact of MSX and Dermo Disease on Oyster Stocks in the Northeast Region," Northeastern Regional Aquaculture Center, NRAC Fact Sheet No. 200, 1993.

132. Ibid.

133. DATA SOURCE: National Marine Fisheries Service, http://www.st.nmfs.noaa.gov/commercial-fisheries/commercial-landings/annual-landings/.

134. Ibid.

135. Tom Horton, "For Skipjack Captains, the Oyster Is Their World," *Baltimore Sun*, October 24, 1992.

136. Thomas J. Murray and James E. Kirkley, "Economic Activity Associated with Clam Aquaculture in Virginia," Department of Fisheries Science, Virginia Institute of Marine Science, July 2005.

137. Heather Dewar, Tommy Landers and Elizabeth Ridlington, "Watermen Blues: Economic, Cultural and Community Impacts of Poor Water Quality in the Chesapeake Bay," Environment Maryland Research and Policy Center, September 2009.

138. Brett R. Dumbauld, Jennifer Ruesink and Steven S. Rumrill, "The Ecological Role of Bivalve Shellfish Aquaculture in the Estuarine Environment," *Aquaculture* (February 2009).

139. Merrill Leffler and Jack Greer, "The Ecology of *Crassostrea gigas* in Australia, New Zealand, France, and Washington State," scientific paper, Maryland Sea Grant College, 1991.

140. Guy Leonard, "Watermen See Hope in Asian Oyster, but Little Action," *Southern Maryland Headline News*, February 17, 2009.

141. Lawrence Latane III, "Maryland Wary of Asian Oyster, Virginia, Hoping to Save Industry, OK's More Tests," *Richmond Times-Dispatch*, May 29, 2001.

142. Associated Press, "Trade Group Pushes Large Aquaculture Plan Using Sterile Oysters," *Chesapeake Bay Journal*, April 1, 2008.

143. Gail Dean, "Watermen Speak Up for Asian Oysters in Bay," www.myeasternshoremd.com, November 21, 2008.

144. Ibid.

145. Janet Krenn, "Selecting a Better Oyster (Part 2): Back From the Brink," Vaseagrant.vims.edu, May 8, 2013.

146. Karl Blankenship, "Introduction of Oysters Too Risky for Bay," *Chesapeake Bay Journal*, May 1, 2009.

147. Michael Fincham, writer/producer, *An Oyster Inventor and His Quest* [Motion picture]. Baltimore, Maryland. Maryland Sea Grant, 2010.

148. Dean, "Watermen Speak Up."

149. Karen Hudson, Dan Kauffman, Thomas J. Murray and Alexander Solomon, "2012 Cultchless (Single Seed) Oyster Crop Budgets for Virginia," Virginia Institute of Marine Science, Virginia Sea Grant Marine Extension Program, November 2012.

150. Karen Hudson and Thomas J. Murray, "Virginia Shellfish Aquaculture Situation and Outlook Report, 2013," Virginia Sea Grant Marine Extension Program, Virginia Institute of Marine Science, 2013.

151. Ibid.

152. Rona Kobell, "Aquaculture Most Likely Future for Bay's Oysters," *Chesapeake Bay Journal*, October 1, 2010.

153. Karl Blankenship, "Panel Says Future of Bay Oyster Likely to Be Aquaculture, Large Sanctuaries," *Chesapeake Bay Journal*, February 1, 2008.
154. Wheeler, "O'Malley Plans to Limit Oyster Harvest."
155. Kobell, "Aquaculture Most Likely Future."
156. "Support Maryland Watermen," Facebook page (accessed May 13, 2014).

## CHAPTER 9

157. Karen Hudson and Thomas J. Murray, "Virginia Shellfish Aquaculture Situation and Outlook Report," VIMS, Virginia Sea Grant Extension Program, 2014.
158. Janine Stewart, "Entrepreneur-Driven US Oyster Industry Growing on Farm-to-Table Movement," *Undercurrent News*, January 27, 2014.

# INDEX

# ABOUT THE AUTHOR

K ate Livie is a professional Chesapeake educator, writer and historian. She is also an Eastern Shore native and currently serves as director of education at the Chesapeake Bay Maritime Museum in St. Michaels, Maryland. Livie is a passionate advocate for the Chesapeake Bay's culture, heritage and landscape and

considers herself lucky to live in a place so endlessly beautiful and fascinating. Livie resides with her husband, Ben, on Morgan Creek in Chestertown, Maryland. To date, she owns thirteen oyster knives and has mastered shucking from the hinge but is working on her bill shucking technique.